Praise for The *Elegant* Pitch

"Mike Figliuolo has delivered a practical approach that leaders at any level can use to hone their persuasive communication skills and get buy-in for ideas. The ability to exude 'executive presence' often determines whether or not your career advances. So many people receive ambiguous feedback that they have to improve their 'executive presence' but are left to figure out for themselves what that means. A core aspect of true executive presence is the ability to share your thoughts in a simple, persuasive way. **The Elegant Pitch** provides a proven method for demonstrating this elusive skill. We've used these concepts to groom our high-potential leaders at Cardinal Health and received great feedback on the techniques. Mike's Structured Thought & Communications training improved their confidence, strengthened their executive presence, and enabled them to deliver a strong message with impact. I highly recommend this book."

—Lisa George,
formerly Vice President, Global Talent Management,
Cardinal Health; now Vice President,
International Talent, Walmart

"One of the most important skills needed in the workplace today is the ability to tell a story to gain support for your idea. But this is a skill that few seem to have or are able to hone. Mike Figliuolo's latest book, **The Elegant Pitch**, provides you with the mechanics of the perfect pitch and offers creative techniques for delivering it. And as always, Mike writes with wit and humor. This is that one book that you will read, re-read, and recommend to others. I know what book my department book club will be reading next!"

"If you need to frame up situations, challenges, and decision paths or you're looking for support, budget, and headcount for your ideas, you'll want to read this book twice. The first pass will be an entertaining read where you 'see' yourself in the stories Mike tells. In the second read you'll see how his approach can get you the support you're seeking for your ideas. Here's to mastery of the Elegant Pitch. Well done, Mike."

"Mike Figliuolo has created another 'must read' for the business world with his latest book, **The Elegant Pitch**. Based on his Structured Thought & Communications course, Mike provides a practical roadmap and tools to improve your persuasive communications and increase your influencing capabilities. If you want to get to better decisions faster, have fewer and more productive meetings, and drive greater alignment, read this book and apply the methods it contains."

"**The Elegant Pitch** outlines a commonsense—yet rarely followed—approach that can help anyone in business increase their impact and be more influential. This book takes the successful methods used by management consultants and applies them to everyday business situations. The outcome is a method that can lead to outstanding results. I would recommend **The Elegant Pitch** to any of my business leaders or mentees."

—Katie Liebel,
Senior Vice President, Transformation,
Nationwide

The
Elegant
Pitch

The
Elegant
Pitch

- → Create a Compelling Recommendation,
- → Build Broad Support,
- → And Get It Approved

MIKE FIGLIUOLO

coauthor of *Lead Inside the Box*

CAREER
PRESS
Pompton Plains, N.J.

THE ELEGANT PITCH
EDITED BY LAUREN MANOY
TYPESET BY KARA KUMPEL
Cover design by Jeff Piasky
Pen photo: koosen/shutterstock
Printed in the U.S.A.

To order this title, please call toll-free 1-800-CAREER-1 (NJ and Canada: 201-848-0310) to order using VISA or MasterCard, or for further information on books from Career Press.

The Career Press, Inc.
12 Parish Drive
Wayne, NJ 07470
www.careerpress.com

Library of Congress Cataloging-in-Publication Data

CIP Data Available Upon Request.

∞

ÖÖ

Acknowledgments

I'm writing this book for all those I haven't thanked in my prior works. Your love, support, friendship, guidance, patience, and understanding make everything I do possible. Thank you. For everything.

Danielle, Michael, and Alexandra, thank you for the continued smiles. But not the gray hairs. Those suck. That said, you know I'll *always* be there for you. No matter what. Even at 3 A.M. on a Friday night.

Mom and Dad, your love and support mean more than you'll ever know.

Gina, I'm sorry. You're fine. You're fine. Please don't tell Mom.

Nana, Pop, Grandma, and Grandpa, I miss you guys. Thanks for all the wonderful gifts you gave me when you were with us.

Giles Anderson, for your expertise at peeling me off the ceiling as needed.

Adam Schwartz and the Career Press team, thanks for giving me another chance to share my ideas with the world.

My McKinsey colleagues, for teaching me how to communicate and influence others. Without you, this book and my business aren't possible.

Cecilia Frew, first, for teaching me how to do this stuff, and second, for giving me my first chance to make a living at it.

Paul Zamecnik, for encouraging me to teach this method and recognizing it as a gift I could give to others.

Everyone who's participated in my courses, thank you for making teaching a joy. For engaging with the content. For getting me invited back. It's a pleasure working with each and every one of you.

Contents

Introduction

One of the most challenging tasks any professional faces is getting a recommendation approved. People pitch ideas every day. You would think they'd get good at it after all that practice. The puzzling part is, they don't. The reason all their practice doesn't improve their communication skills is they're not *practicing* their communication skills. All too often they're practicing their analysis skills. Most of their effort is spent on running numbers, creating complex graphs, and churning out massive presentations designed to impress their audience with how rigorous they've been. That approach is broken. Audiences don't have the time or the patience to wade through ponderous reports. They want an answer, and they want it *now*!

Add to this challenge the complexity of the matrixed environments people operate in where competing agendas are the norm. No matter what's being recommended, someone will be upset about it. It's difficult to build support across stakeholders, let alone do so in an efficient way.

When the pitch bores the audience and causes conflict among stakeholders, decisions never get made and approval is never granted. The cycle repeats itself as the person making the pitch rushes off to complete more analysis to satisfy all the issues that emerged during the meeting. Unfortunately, that extra analysis never seems to satisfy everyone's concerns and the cycle continues unbroken.

We can only break out of this dysfunctional dynamic by changing the way we approach making a pitch. Instead of putting data and analysis first, we should think through our argument and how we'll make our case. We need to consider stakeholder concerns before we start running numbers. We should build support for the idea well in advance of any decision meeting. When we shift our thinking and work through the logic before we work through the numbers, we can get our pitch approved much more efficiently.

The method I'll share in this book is fundamentally different than the "get data, draw conclusion" mindset that's pervasive in most business environments. It's a hypothesis-driven approach designed to focus on the central idea of your pitch and build logical as well as stakeholder support for it. While this approach might be radically different than how you're crafting pitches today, you have to ask yourself: Is the way you're crafting pitches getting you the results you want? If the answer is no, perhaps it's time to try something new to see if you can achieve the outcome you desire—getting your recommendation approved.

The Communication
Challenge

"We're sorry, but your recommendation wasn't approved."

We've all heard those words. It's a sentence that swallows our hopes and crushes our confidence. Why do we get that negative response from our stakeholders? The following scenario illustrates the reasons behind the rejection.

Imagine after weeks of long hours, complex analyses, countless meetings, and earnest lobbying, you take your idea to the steering committee. It's obvious the idea will generate great value for the organization. You pull together the relevant analyses, compile a comprehensive presentation, and polish your slides until they're brilliant. The resultant presentation amounts to fifty-three pages of rigorous data you're sure will impress the committee members.

On the day of the meeting, your excitement is palpable. You've done everything you need to do to make a solid case. There's no way they'll say no to your idea. As you watch copies of your presentation being handed out, you see people flipping through the pages. You think, This is a good sign! They're interested! On closer inspection, though, you see confused looks on their faces. A hand goes up and the steering committee member says, "I have a question on page 42." You nervously flip to the page in question. As you do, you realize you haven't even introduced yourself yet. The audience grows frustrated as you answer their questions. Some committee members ask for more context and others ask why you're covering information they already know. One audience member is intent upon pointing out every flaw in your recommendation in an effort to sabotage your idea. "I don't see how your project drives productivity at all," he says. You wish you had thought to include something on productivity, but you ran out of time to do more analysis.

The thirty minutes you were allotted stretches into a painful forty-five minutes full of questions, complaints, and heavy sighs. Finally, the steering committee chairwoman puts an end to your misery when she says, "I'm sorry. We can't approve this idea today. You'll have to come back next month." With a slump of your shoulders, you take your seat in the back of the room. Your brilliant presentation became a glorious train wreck that sent your idea up in flames.

Your colleague Jillian is the next presenter. You feel bad for her because she only has fifteen minutes to talk because your presentation chewed up half of her time. On top of that, you've riled up the crowd. Now she's forced to speak in front of an irritated audience. She passes around a short, nine-page presentation. "She's going to get crushed! She has almost no supporting information for her idea," you think to yourself.

She clears her throat and says, "If everyone could please turn to the executive summary, I'd like to highlight a few points. Today I'm recommending we launch a new communications training program. The main takeaway is: if we save one hour per person, per month through improved communication efficiency, we save $350,000 per year in improved productivity." You see the committee members' heads nodding in agreement as they read along with her summary while Jillian stands there in silence. Once they finish reading, they turn their eyes to her again.

Jillian asks, "Does anyone have any questions? I know we have limited time, so I'd like to keep our discussion focused on points of concern."

"I'm good with everything up to this fifth bullet point where you cover the productivity improvement," says the same committee member who badgered you about productivity during your presentation. You're eager to see how Jillian defends herself from his oncoming attack.

"I understand your concern. If it's okay with everyone, please turn to page 6." Jillian advances her slides to her savings analysis.

You shake your head and think, I can't believe this. She's skipping so many pages. Her idea will never get approved this way.

Jillian explains her productivity savings calculations then asks, "Are there any other questions?" Everyone shakes their head in the negative. "Okay, if everyone could please turn to page 9, I'd like to discuss approval, expenditure authorization, and next steps." She walks the committee through her funding request and explains the timeline for rolling out the training. When she finishes, she turns her attention to the steering committee chairwoman.

The chairwoman's response leaves you slack-jawed. "This is an exciting program, Jillian. Personally, I love the productivity improvements we'll get from it." She then asks the audience, "Are we all in agreement with rolling this out?"

Heads nod in the affirmative around the table.

The chairwoman continues, "It looks like we all support your idea. Consider this your approval to launch the program. Please update us once the program enters the rollout phase." Jillian thanks the committee and leaves the room having used fourteen of her fifteen minutes.

She only talked about *three pages* and got her idea approved! How did she do that? you wonder in silent awe.

The answer is simple: Jillian used a straightforward process for defining her idea, building her argument, and sharing the most relevant information with her audience. She thought about her objectives, her audience's goals, and how to best structure her pitch before she did any analysis, let alone create any slides in a presentation. She focused on the desired outcome—getting her idea approved—instead of how pretty her visuals were or how impressive her analysis was. By keeping the end in mind, she was able to let go of her own agenda and go where the audience needed to go.

An *Efficient* Method for Communicating Effectively

This is a learnable skill. It's simpler than you might believe. I call it the **structured thought process**. When done correctly, you'll be able to go from basic idea to approved recommendation more efficiently and effectively than you thought was possible. To learn how to do this, you'll need to abandon usual behaviors and be open to techniques that will be intellectually uncomfortable. At first this process may feel backwards. You may even look at the process and think, That can never work, especially in my organization. These are natural reactions to learning something counter to what you've been taught in the past. Once you get past those hang-ups and drop your bad habits, you'll find this process is intuitive and full of common sense. The reason we have trouble using this method is because we mistakenly believe it's too simple to be effective. The method's beauty is its simplicity and elegance.

The word "elegant" might seem like an odd choice to describe making a business pitch, but I chose it because of a meaningful experience I had early in my career. I was new to the company and was responsible for several business areas. Our executive vice president (EVP) wanted to get a better understanding of all the projects her teams were working on. My presentation would be my first interaction with her in any way. It was an important conversation because she was my boss's boss's boss's boss.

This first impression I made upon her could have a large impact—positive or negative—on my team, my performance reviews, and my career.

I spent days honing my presentation using the method I describe in this book. I ensured my story was compelling. Every word and image I used was meaningful. I conducted several rounds of conversations with stakeholders to get their input on my work. When I presented to our EVP, the conversation went smoothly. She was able to follow along and get a clear understanding of my business areas in a short period of time. After I finished presenting, I asked if she had any questions. Her response sticks with me to this day. She said, "It's all clear. That was an elegant presentation. It flowed because it was straightforward and easy to understand. No questions. Good stuff. Thanks." That was all she had to say. I couldn't think of any higher praise for my work. All the time I had spent preparing the presentation paid off because my audience got the message, didn't get distracted by extraneous information, and she was able to understand what was going on in my areas of responsibility. That was the day I decided I wanted to make every pitch I gave live up to the compliment of being elegant. I'd like to provide you the same set of tools I used so you can make your pitches elegant too.

This is the same method used by elite global-strategy consulting firms to make their most challenging recommendations. It's a hypothesis-driven approach designed to arrive at fact-based, data-driven recommendations in short periods of time. The recommendations these organizations make are subject to significant scrutiny. By following the method, people advancing these ideas are able to identify stakeholder objectives, understand their points of resistance or support, craft a compelling narrative, bring the right data to the table, and make a convincing case that's approved the first time it's presented. This method isn't reserved for those consulting firms, nor is it restricted to consulting engagements. You can use it in your day-to-day work for any recommendation you're making.

The method is flexible. While it's typically used for making recommendations in a slide presentation, this process can be used as effectively for writing emails, business cases, and memos. You can use the method when leaving voicemails, or in direct conversations in person or on the phone. The approach is as relevant for delivering a status update as it is for making a business case. You can improve any situation requiring you to communicate with someone else for the purpose of conveying information and influencing them by using this method.

Make no mistake, the method is simple but applying it is challenging. As you read this book, you might have the reaction of wow, that's easy. Then when you apply the method you'll see how difficult it can be. Why? Because you have to *think*. A lot. The seventeenth-century French logician and mathematician Blaise Pascal said, "I would have written a shorter letter but I did not have the time." Why does it take longer to write a shorter letter? Because you have to *think*. Pascal understood the effort required to hone a message to be clear, concise, and compelling. You need to achieve the same outcome with your communications. This method is how you can do it.

What's in It for You

I'm asking you to change long-ingrained behaviors, manage through organizational resistance, and build a difficult new skill with the precious little time you have available. For you to go to all that trouble, there has to be a payoff. The method's benefits are:

Clearer and more compelling recommendations. This method defines your recommendation precisely. It forces you to understand your audience's goals then link your pitch to those goals. When you do so, your recommendation will be easier to understand and your audience should support it.

Shorter and crisper communications. Using this process results in your audience spending less time reading the communication. You'll spend less time answering clarifying questions because there won't be as many questions to answer. A nine-page presentation is easier to read than a ninety-page one. It's less confusing when it's written well. Stripping out extraneous information to create a shorter narrative results in fewer possible points of confusion and therefore fewer questions. This means less back-and-forth discussion in search of clarity.

Greater analytical efficiency. This benefit comes in the form of doing less "junk" analysis and focusing instead on gathering the facts *required* to make your pitch. The method will tell you what information you need to support your recommendation. Correspondingly, the method will identify extraneous information and unnecessary analysis. You'll avoid wasting time on analysis that will never see the light of day.

Fewer and shorter meetings. You'll spend less time in meetings because there are fewer questions and less re-work. Participants will be clearer about what your recommendation is and why you're pursuing it. You'll have the right information with you during the first meeting rather than entering the endless loop of continuous requests for additional information. Getting your pitch right the first time means all the follow-on meetings never have to happen.

More efficient decision-making processes. Your teams can make decisions the first time you meet because the right information is available and it's shared in a straightforward narrative. The method builds buy-in as you're creating your narrative. By the time you get to the final meeting, you'll have answered everyone's big questions and you'll know what information to share to get your final approval.

A higher likelihood of getting your pitch approved. You won't get a yes every time you use this method, but you will get approval more frequently. People will understand what you're asking for and why they should support your idea. You'll bring the right data to the conversation, and you'll be prepared to handle objections as they arise. If you bring the right data and address all stakeholder concerns, approval is a logical outcome.

Do less work, have fewer and shorter meetings, and get pitches approved on the first pass. Sign me up! In all seriousness, this method delivers those benefits if you're rigorous about applying these skills on a consistent basis.

How to *Use* This Book

Over the course of this book, I'll explain the method and how it works. I'll then break down each step in the process and offer examples of what the output of that step looks like. Along the way I'll share useful tips so you can master this method. I'll also point out pitfalls that can derail your efforts. I encourage you to select pitches you're working on and apply each step of the method to that recommendation as you work your way through the book. Conducting that exercise will translate the concepts herein to real-world application.

Please recognize this process is messy and you won't have the right answer at every step. In fact, when I teach this course to clients, I often tell people to embrace the wrong. During the early steps of the method, your answers will be wrong. That's okay. This method isn't about being right every step of the way. It's about iterating and taking one step closer to the correct answer, recognizing that might mean changing work you did in a previous step. I ask you to not be frustrated by that dynamic but instead to accept it. Each iteration results in you getting closer to your final answer. If you go into this process with a mindset of having a perfect end product each step of the way, you'll become disillusioned, give up, and revert to old habits.

This book isn't about how to use PowerPoint, Prezi, Keynote, or any other presentation software. It's about all the thinking you should do *before* you open any of those programs. Writing a presentation by starting in presentation software is a trap. Don't worry, I'll cover how all the thinking you do in the method is turned into a presentation—if that's the correct communication vehicle. For now, set aside your questions about how to create a slide presentation.

This method is about conveying the *right* information, not *all* the information. Your ability to simplify your message and select the most relevant facts is at the heart of your successful application of this method. Don't be afraid to leave information out of the conversation. If someone has a question, you can always answer it later. The better you get at simplifying your message, the more likely it is to be supported. Pythagoras captured this method's essence best when he said, "Do not say a little in many words, but a great deal in few." If you follow the method and heed his advice, the few words you do share will drive the outcome you desire—getting the idea you're pitching approved!

The *Structured* Thought Process

Before you learn a new way to think, you must understand the current approach for generating recommendations. Once you see how the current process falls short, the new process I'm advocating will make more sense in terms of the rationale for why the steps are sequenced the way they are. Most people I work with on building this skill approach their work in what seems to be a logical way. When they're asked to make a recommendation, they follow this approach:

Step 1: Gather large amounts of data and do excessive amounts of analysis.

Step 2: Look for insights emerging from said analysis.

Step 3: Assemble all the analysis into a comprehensive document to demonstrate how rigorous they've been.

Step 4: Share a thirty- to sixty-page document in a two-hour-long meeting thinking they'll impress their audience with the depths of their insights.

Unfortunately, step 5 consists of the audience being confused to the point that they don't approve the recommendation. Instead, they request a follow-up meeting to review the idea again. The worst part is, the person making the recommendation goes into round two with even *more* data. They add information under the mistaken assumption that their idea wasn't approved because they didn't have enough analysis supporting it.

The real reason it wasn't approved was the audience didn't understand the recommendation in the first place. There was no clear narrative to guide them from their current understanding of the situation to a place where the recommendation made sense. They were overwhelmed by analyses that didn't present a coherent story they could digest in a matter of minutes. This dynamic is bad enough at the manager level. The situation gets worse at executive levels. There's a reason communicating at senior levels is difficult. I call it Figliuolo's Law, which states:

An individual's annual compensation is inversely proportional to the number of slides they can look at before they have a stroke.

The more senior an individual is, the less time they have for detailed explanations. They want the top level answer. They trust your competence; that's why they hired you. They know if they have questions, you'll be able to walk them through the detail. What they're looking for when you make a pitch to them is a narrative that quickly tells them what the recommendation is, why it makes sense, and what you need to make it happen. Long presentations frustrate them. I worked with one CEO who used to say, "If your recommendation has a staple in it, I won't read it." You had to get your message across to him on a single page no matter how big the recommendation was!

I worked with another CEO who personified Figliuolo's Law. One day my team went in to present to him along with another team. The other team presented first. They handed him their twenty-five-page presentation. Before they even opened their mouths to speak, the CEO picked up their presentation and motioned as if he was weighing it. He then threw their slides across the room and snapped, "Talk to me! What do you want? I'm busy. I don't have time for all this paper." They were surprised. We weren't. We knew better, and our presentation was three pages long. The difference between our approach and theirs was their intent was to share everything they knew. Our intent was to share what our CEO *needed to know* to make a decision.

The common practice of going from data to analysis to presentation is broken. It's an inefficient process because most of the analysis will never see the light of day. It's wasted effort. When your meetings don't go well because you tried to cram forty pages of content into a thirty-minute meeting, you've wasted everyone's time— not only in that meeting, but also in the one you create to reconvene and discuss the idea again. Yay! Another meeting! People who continue to use this approach lose credibility. They're perceived as lacking executive presence because they ramble through their analyses. Their results suffer because they never get their ideas approved in the first place. This madness has to stop.

A *New* Approach

I'm going to ask you to do something completely backward. The **structured thought process** begins with the answer then works to prove or disprove it. The sequence of steps in the process is deliberate. Don't jump ahead or do the steps out of order, or you'll cause issues for yourself. The process is shown on the next page.

➴

Here's a short description of each step. I'll explain each step in great detail in future chapters.

Step 1: Define the question. You have to understand what the problem is before you can solve it. Get clarity from your requestor as to what the issue is and why they want it solved.

Step 2: Create a core idea. The core idea is your primary recommendation. It spells out the action you want to take and the rationale for taking the action. The core idea is a hypothesis as to what the recommendation could be combined with a reason for pursuing it. That reason must be something of value *to your audience.*

Step 3: Build the architecture. The logic of your argument is the architecture. It's how you're going to arrange your facts and analyses to support your core idea.

Step 4: Create the story. The story is your simple narrative that gets your audience to arrive at your conclusion. It's derived from your architecture.

Figure 2.1: The Structured Thought Process

Step 5: Discuss and refine the story. This is where you get other people's feedback on your idea. Notice you're involving others well before you expend effort on analysis.

Step 6: Select core facts and analyses. This method isn't about having *all* the facts. It's about having the *right* facts. The facts and analyses you choose to do will be gathered to support your architecture.

Step 7: Prove or disprove the hypothesis. The analysis you perform is done with the purpose of proving or disproving your hypothesis. This focus on *required* analysis is what makes the method efficient.

Step 8: Finalize the communication. Whether you're creating a presentation, a memo, an email, or any other document, you won't assemble it until the process's final stages. By the time you reach this step, your entire document is already written. This step is an exercise in assembly.

Step 9: Share the idea. Ultimately, you will share your idea with your stakeholders. Understanding their preferences for how they like to receive information will go a long way toward generating a successful communication.

If those steps look familiar, you may remember them from middle school. This process is a simplified version of the scientific method. You start with a line of inquiry, generate a hypothesis as to what will happen in your experiment, conduct the experiment and gather data, determine if your hypothesis is proven or disproven, then write and share your lab report. I know there are differences between the more rigorous scientific method used in organizations conducting research, but the approach is generally the same. This is the part that's backward:

You start with the answer then get the data to prove or disprove it. That's counter to the way many organizations work. They instead start with vast amounts of data and look for answers to emerge through their analysis. I acknowledge there are times for exploratory analysis where you play with data to get an understanding of it and look for any insights therein. That technique has its place, but the structured thought process has many benefits over using that exploratory analysis approach for everything—especially when you're looking to make a recommendation efficiently.

The structured thought process will make your life easier. It's an efficient way to gather facts because the method guides you to the facts you need and prevents you from wasting time on analyzing those you don't. You'll spend less time on rework because you're syndicating your idea at multiple points in the process. This syndication keeps you from wasted efforts like answering the wrong question or not knowing about major obstacles to your recommendation until you present at the final approval meeting. The process shows you how to kill off low-value ideas and focus on meaningful ones instead. Your communications will be crisper, clearer, and more compelling. This process will reduce decision-making time and increase the odds of getting your idea approved.

Behaviors to Change

To get all the benefits of the structured thought process, your behaviors must change. I'll wager that when you're asked to create a recommendation, you gravitate toward opening one of two software packages. You'll either open a spreadsheet to begin crunching numbers, or you'll open a presentation application like PowerPoint or Keynote to start creating slides. There's a natural reason many of us have this instinct: We want to get to an answer quickly. That desire leads us to believe we're getting closer to an answer if we manipulate numbers and get results from formulas. We feel we're making progress if content starts to fill our slides. But those beliefs are mistaken. In our rush to get to the answer, we don't ensure we're answering the right *question*. Many times we don't even know what the question is; we only have a vague sense of it, or even worse, we misinterpreted the question as we rushed out of our boss's office to go crunch numbers. When we pull together a presentation without having spoken to stakeholders, we might find we did redundant work analyzing a question someone else in the organization answered last month. The rush to an answer makes us less efficient because of all the wasted effort.

Rather than rushing off to open spreadsheets and create slides, find a whiteboard, flip chart, or scratch paper. During the early stages of the structured thought process, your thoughts and the corresponding documents will be messy. Your recommendation will be ambiguous at that stage. It will change as you go through the process. Don't obsess about being right in these early steps. Instead, focus on generating something you can feed into the next step. Don't worry—as your idea moves through the process, it will become clearer. Here are the behaviors I recommend as you go through each step:

Step 1: Define the question. Write your question on scratch paper or a whiteboard. You'll refine it as you discuss it with your requestor and other team members.

Step 2: Create a core idea. This goes on scratch paper too. Don't worry about having the right answer at this stage. You only need to have *an* answer to begin your exploration.

Step 3: Build the architecture. You're best served to draw your architecture on a whiteboard. Those drawings let you visualize your structure. Because your architecture will change as you move through the structured thought process, it's easier to erase and rewrite your thoughts on a whiteboard than it is on a flip chart or scratch paper.

Step 4: Create the story. Create your story in a program like Word or even in an email. Your story will be more of an outline than it will be prose. You'll edit it based on feedback you receive in future process steps.

Step 5: Discuss and refine the story. Send calendar invitations for this step. You'll need to meet with people and get their feedback on your story. A scheduled meeting ensures you have their undivided attention.

Step 6: Select core facts and analyses. Go back to your whiteboard, review your architecture, and create a list of facts and analyses required to prove your case.

Step 7: Prove or disprove the hypothesis. Now you get to pull data, open spreadsheets, and crunch numbers—but you'll do that analysis with a purpose. This isn't exploratory analysis. It's analysis focused on a specific outcome. You'll prove or disprove your idea.

Step 8: Finalize the communication. This is where you create your slides if you're building a presentation. If you're writing a memo or an email, you'll create it in a corresponding program. Choose a communication vehicle appropriate to your audience.

Step 9: Share the idea. The approach you use will be audience dependent. You might choose a formal presentation, a webinar, a conference call, or any other audience-appropriate technique to convey your final recommendation.

When you start using the structured thought process, the early steps will be intellectually uncomfortable. Few people enjoy ambiguity. You might feel like you're not making progress toward generating a recommendation while you're flailing away at a whiteboard or on scratch paper. The more you use the structured thought process, the more you'll come to trust it and learn how critical those early steps are. If you do those first steps well, the ones that follow are easier. When you do begin your analysis, you'll be doing the *right* analyses rather than *all* the analyses.

To get the benefits of the process, you must change your behaviors. I suggest bookmarking this page and keeping it handy. The next time you apply the structured thought process, refer back to these steps. Ask yourself: Am I in a spreadsheet when I should be at the whiteboard? Am I creating slides before I've written my story? If you're not using the recommended techniques, recognize you've fallen into old ways, then change your behavior to follow the process. Over time, these behaviors will become second nature, and you'll get through the structured thought process quickly and efficiently.

Iterate, Iterate, Iterate

While the Structured Thought Process steps follow a sequence, you will iterate multiple times as you advance an idea through these steps. Don't resist going back to a prior step when you learn something new. These iterations will refine your idea, deliver a better answer, and build support for your pitch along the way. You'll find yourself iterating more frequently during step 5 (discuss and refine the story) and step 7 (prove or disprove the hypothesis). For the former, this occurs because when you solicit feedback from others, they provide it. They might tell you that you're answering the wrong question, your architecture doesn't make sense, or your story doesn't flow. They'll raise concerns you hadn't thought of but that you must account for in your final recommendation. You'll need to revisit prior steps to incorporate their feedback as appropriate.

In the latter step of proving or disproving the hypothesis, you will find the data don't always do what you want the data to do. Sometimes you'll think the data will be positive, but when you run the analysis, you find the opposite is true. You'll need to go back to prior steps in the structured thought process and refine your idea to reflect the reality of the data.

This iteration process can be challenging. You'll be sharing incomplete work with others in an attempt to get their feedback. This is another reason I suggest capturing ideas on a whiteboard or scratch paper. When you go to a stakeholder with a draft analysis or a partially completed presentation—even one with dummy data plugged into it—stakeholders perceive you're further along in your work than you truly are. They'll have a tendency to ask about the numbers or make suggestions about slide layout when the feedback you need is whether or not you've drafted a logical argument or a story that flows. They'll think you're closer to an answer than you actually are. If instead you bring them into a team room and show them your architecture handwritten on a whiteboard, they'll understand you're not far along into the process of building your recommendation. Their feedback will focus on your argument's structure, which is where you want their attention.

With every iteration, you're honing your idea. Every piece of feedback you receive brings a stakeholder into the fold and addresses their concerns before the final meeting. Their involvement builds support for your recommendation while you're still writing it. Every analytical iteration brings you closer to a correct answer. The data will point you in the right direction as long as you're willing to listen to what the data are telling you. By the time you've iterated through the process several times, you've already written and bulletproofed your final communication long before it goes to your approving authority. I know it sounds like this process takes time. It can. Iteration is a natural part of the process and it makes your recommendation stronger. While this can be time consuming, iterating is more efficient than continuously getting wrong answers, confusing stakeholders, and reworking your idea several times over.

Start Directionally and End Precisely

When using the structured thought process, adopt a mindset of starting directionally and ending precisely. The early process steps should guide you in a general direction of where the answer lies. As you go through the process, your answer will become more and more precise. For this to work, trust the process. Here's an illustration of how you can go from directional to precise. I've laid out the process steps along with example output from that step. There's accompanying commentary about how that end product was derived or the implications of that end product for future process steps. Pay attention to how the recommendation gets refined as it moves from one step to the next.

Imagine the vice president of sales drops by our team area and says, "I've been thinking about growth plans for the next few years. I'd like your team to get me a recommendation for how we can grow the business in a meaningful way." We decide to try to satisfy her request by using the structured thought process.

Step 1: Define the question. This is a sales issue, therefore we should ignore ideas related to reducing costs. To satisfy our requestor, we have to *increase* sales versus keeping sales flat, despite a competitive environment. The initial question will be broad in scope but it will serve to set direction for our problem solving. Our initial question becomes: "What should we do to increase sales?"

Step 2: Create a core idea. We brainstorm ideas as a team. One idea rises to the top of our list because it seems larger than the others. That idea is expanding our business into Europe because we can achieve $5MM to $100MM in incremental sales. This is a *preliminary* recommendation based upon several directional hypotheses. First, we're hypothesizing we should open locations versus launching new products, expanding existing markets, raising prices, or other growth opportunities. Second, we're hypothesizing we should do this in Europe. That takes Asia, the Americas, Africa, Australia, and Antarctica out of scope. Third, we're hypothesizing as to the range of sales impact. While $5MM to $100MM is a huge range, we know the idea is worth at least $5MM.

That's a "back of the envelope" calculation. We'll refine those numbers later. That $5MM is big enough for us to continue taking the idea through the structured thought process. When we make a recommendation to the Vice President of sales, we should tell her how many sales dollars we're going to generate because she cares about that metric more than others. Our preliminary core idea becomes: "We should open new locations in Europe to generate $5MM to $100MM in sales."

Step 3: Build the architecture. To support our core idea, our architecture must prove that we're able to open new locations, that Europe is attractive, and that we can generate substantial sales revenue. These three points will need to be proven for our recommendation to be supported. We don't yet know if these three supports are correct. We'll figure out if they're correct or not later in the process. All these points will be supported with additional detail as the architecture gets refined. For now, we're hypothesizing that these proof points will be true and therefore support our recommendation. The main points of our architecture become: We have the ability to open new locations; Europe is an attractive market; and we can generate significant sales volume.

Step 4: Create the story. The story will capture the flow of our argument in the form of a simple narrative. It is designed to shape the reader's perspective and guide them through the supporting information with the goal of drawing the right conclusion. The story is a draft, so it won't have a lot of detail at this stage. It will be more of an outline of our thinking in the form of a few bullet points. Our initial story could be the following:

We should open new locations in Europe to generate $5MM to $100MM in sales.

➢ We have the ability to open new locations because we've successfully done so in the past.

➢ Europe is an attractive market because it's growing and underpenetrated.

➢ We can generate significant sales volume if we enter the European market.

The points in our story need more support and ultimately need to be proven with facts and data. For now, we've captured a rough flow of our logic.

Step 5: Discuss and refine the story. As we discuss our story with others and get their input, they help us scope how many locations we should evaluate, point us to countries with large opportunities, steer us away from less attractive ones, and offer high-level thoughts on how big the sales opportunity is. Our refined core idea becomes: "We should open five to ten new locations in Italy, Germany, and France to generate $18MM to $30MM in sales."

Step 6: Select core facts and analyses. We need to analyze how many locations to open and confirm we have the capability to open them. We must analyze the Italian, German, and French markets to ensure they're attractive. We'll conduct the financial analysis to determine how much revenue we can expect from each market. Every analysis on our list is derived from points we need to prove in our architecture. There are hundreds of analyses we *won't* perform because they don't contribute to proving or disproving our recommendation. Avoiding those irrelevant analyses will save us time.

Step 7: Prove or disprove the hypothesis. Our analysis indicates the French market isn't as attractive as we thought. Other analyses further refine the size of the sales opportunity in Italy and Germany. Those analyses give us a better sense for how many locations we need to open to achieve those sales goals. The results of our analyses make our recommendation more precise. Our core idea becomes: "We should open seven or eight new locations in Italy and Germany to generate $19MM to $23MM in sales."

Step 8: Finalize the communication. We construct a seven-page slide presentation:

- ∞ Page 1 is the title page.
- ∞ Page 2 is the executive summary.
- ∞ Page 3 covers opening seven or eight new locations.
- ∞ Pages 4 and 5 explain the Italian and the German market opportunities.
- ∞ Page 6 lays out the pro forma sales projections.
- ∞ Page 7 explains the next steps required to launch the initiative.

That's it. Seven pages. Every page serves to advance the recommendation. Sure there will be backup analyses and pages on points like why France isn't an attractive market, deeper sales projections, and market research, but that information doesn't need to be included in the main presentation. It's there in case someone asks for additional detail.

Step 9: Share the idea. We discuss our recommendation with our stakeholder—the Vice President of sales—in a one-hour meeting. She understands the recommendation and our rationale for making it. She asks one question about why we excluded France, which we answer with a slide from the appendix. After receiving that answer, she approves our idea. We begin deeper planning and analysis in support of the market entry as we implement the plan.

When we started the process, the answer was broad and ambiguous: increase sales. As we moved through the process, we refined our recommendation based on conversations, analysis, and new information. We focused on what was meaningful by analyzing the points required to make our case and ignoring analyses that would distract us. The result was a clear, concise recommendation tailored to meet the needs of a specific stakeholder. The outcome was what we wanted—approval for our recommendation. This was a simplified example designed to give you a sense of how an idea evolves as it moves through the process. I omitted most of the iteration you'll do in the real world for the sake of making this example easy to understand.

Using the structured thought process isn't easy. It requires discipline because you must avoid the temptation to do analysis or build slides until late in the process. The method requires determination and patience because you'll work through multiple iterations of your idea before arriving at your ultimate conclusion. Even then there's no guarantee your idea will be approved on the first pass. But if you're rigorous about following the process and you get comfortable with moving from ambiguity to precision, you'll be pitching more compelling recommendations more efficiently than you ever thought was possible.

3

Define the *Question* and Create *Hypotheses*

The first step in the structured thought process is to define the question. All too often when stakeholders ask for a recommendation, we rush off to conduct analysis and bring back an idea as quickly as possible. That approach can cause massive problems because we never stop to get clarity on what the real issue is. Teams often assume everyone knows what the question is and therefore don't take the time to document the issue. Even if they do document the issue, they don't go the extra step of explaining *why* it's important to the stakeholder to solve the issue. Without clarity and agreement on the "what" and the "why" of the issue, the likelihood of generating a recommendation that will meet the stakeholder's needs is low.

To demonstrate the importance of defining and documenting the question, let's walk through an example. Imagine I'm your stakeholder and I ask you for a recommendation. I ask, "Can you get me your best idea for how we can generate an incremental $1MM in profits? Thanks!" Then I leave the room. For this exercise, write down the first three ideas that come to mind for how you can solve my problem. Go ahead, write them down so we can refer back to them.

Finished? Okay, let's look at your ideas. You may have come up with ones like launching a new product, entering a new market, reducing manufacturing costs, conducting a layoff, or raising prices. You might want to launch a new marketing campaign, set up a joint venture, offer discounts to drive sales, or cut travel expenses. These are great ideas, but you might have a big problem. Your ideas might satisfy my "what," but you have no idea what my "why" is—the reason I want this solved.

Imagine if my request to you was, "Can you get me your best idea for how we can generate an incremental $1MM in profits *because* our earnings quarter ends in three weeks and we have to make up a financial shortfall? Thanks!" Now look at the list of ideas you generated. Will any of them meet my needs as a stakeholder? Do any get me $1MM in three weeks? If you're lucky, maybe one does, but most likely not. Think about how much effort you could have wasted if you didn't understand my "why," that I need that money in three weeks. You might have conducted a large market and new product analysis, generated ideas for prototypes, and put together a launch plan to get the product to market in a blazing-fast six months. All that analysis took you two weeks to conduct. When you come pitch your idea, instead of being overjoyed with your brilliant new product launch, I'm furious you wasted two of our precious three weeks messing around with irrelevant analysis. Both of us are at fault. I'm culpable because I didn't tell you the "why" of my request. You're at fault because you didn't ask for the "why," and you didn't come back to me to confirm the question that needed to be answered.

Let's change the scenario to one where I ask, "Can you get me your best idea for how we can generate an incremental $1MM in profits because our earnings quarter ends in three weeks and we have to make up a financial shortfall? Thanks!" You know the "why" up front. You'll focus on ideas resulting in short-term profits. You might generate ideas like locking down all corporate travel for three weeks, raising prices across the board, or deferring a large marketing campaign expenditure to the next quarter. Ideas like those will meet my needs and will receive a warmer reception when you pitch them to me. You won't waste time on analysis that doesn't matter. All your energy will focus on helping me achieve my objective. When you build a recommendation that's mindful of the "why," your odds of getting your idea approved increase tremendously.

There are several implications stemming from defining the question. If you're the one asking for ideas, be sure to let your team know the "why" behind your request.

You'll set them up to be successful that way. If you're the one being asked to generate a recommendation and your stakeholder doesn't tell you the "why" of the request, ask them what it is. Let them know you want to meet their needs, and to do so, you have to understand their objectives. Finally, write the question down. This is part of the discipline. By writing it down, you can go back to your stakeholder with something concrete and confirm it's the question they want you to answer. If it's not what they want answered, you'll be able to iterate with them and refine the question until you're both in agreement on what they want you to answer. If you've ever spent a great deal of effort generating a recommendation only to find out on the back end that you answered the wrong question, you'll understand how critical this agreement is.

The *Question* Sets the Direction

A well-articulated question guides you to deliver a recommendation that meets a stakeholder's needs. The question defines the direction of the problem solving by scoping the solution space. Part of this method's efficiency comes from ignoring ideas that are out of scope and focusing on ideas that drive the desired result. For example, look at the scoping implications if your stakeholder asked you for recommendations that satisfy the following question:

How can we decrease Business Unit X's costs to increase corporate gross margin?

While the question may feel broad, your stakeholder has already set a direction for you and managed the scope of your problem solving. First, they've made this a cost-reduction problem. All ideas related to increasing revenues—pricing, marketing, new product launches, and so on—are out of scope. Second, they've asked you to focus on business unit X, so Business Units Y and Z are out of scope. Third, they've told you their objective is to increase gross margin. They're asking you to focus on costs above the gross margin line. Ideas like reducing raw material costs or direct labor costs are in scope, but cutting below the gross margin line costs like corporate travel, legal expenses, IT, and HR are out of scope. Last, you'll need to calculate how much your cost savings will not only improve Business Unit X's gross margin but also to determine how much those savings will improve the *corporate* gross margin. That's a specific analysis that will have to be in your final presentation. They asked a simple question, but its wording has profound implications for how you solve the problem. The solution space is quite large. There are many ideas you can pursue that will meet your stakeholder's needs. At the same time, their question helps you avoid unproductive analyses and ideas. This specificity will save you effort and accelerate your problem solving.

As you begin using the structured thought process, get in the habit of writing your question down, then confirming with your stakeholder that it's the question they want answered. Failure to get their agreement creates the risk you'll wander off into unproductive ideas and wasted analysis. If you skip the step of defining the question, you have a low likelihood of getting your idea approved. Getting agreement on the question during these early stages pays dividends when it comes time to pitch your recommendation.

Hypotheses: *Arguing* About Things You Make Up

The structured thought process is a hypothesis-driven method. A hypothesis is a tentative explanation for an observation, phenomenon, or problem that can be tested by further analysis. In the structured thought process, a hypothesis is something taken to be true for the purpose of argument or investigation. It's the answer to the question you generated in the first step. Essentially, your hypothesis is an answer you make up with the intent of proving or disproving it later. Don't worry, you won't share this answer with stakeholders until later in the process when you've thought the idea through. Some stakeholders won't see your idea until you've proven your case. For now, this is an idea you're generating on scrap paper or a whiteboard. Don't obsess over being right at this stage.

There are several reasons the structured thought process is hypothesis driven. Such an approach will drive to an answer quickly. Your hypothesis will define the information required to prove your argument and indicate which information isn't relevant to your answer. That reduces time spent on wasted analysis. Hypotheses enable you to be fact-based in the pursuit of your answer. The hypothesis allows you to take an educated guess at what the answer will be and then gather facts to prove or disprove that answer. If you prove your hypothesis, it becomes your ultimate recommendation. If you disprove it, you'll go into the iteration process until you find a recommendation you can prove. The crisper your hypothesis, the more likely it is that everyone involved understands the answer and recommendation.

When you generate your hypothesis, be bold! Take a stand by articulating a strong position. This is no time to equivocate. Too often, I see weak hypotheses like, "We should explore XYZ," "We should consider doing X," or "We should analyze ABC." Who's going to say we shouldn't pursue those recommendations? No one. Those are weak hypotheses. They don't push toward an actionable recommendation. The reason people generate weak hypotheses is they're afraid of being wrong. They feel like they're committing to something too early in the process because they don't have any data to back up their hypothesis. You'll need to overcome this fear. The way to get past these concerns is to realize no one will see your early hypothesis and you'll be able to gather data during later steps in the process. A good hypothesis defines a position that can be proven or disproven. "We should open new locations in Europe" is a strong hypothesis. We're taking a stand when we say that. We can gather data later that will tell us if Europe is an attractive market or not. If it is, we've proven our hypothesis and we advance that recommendation. If the data disprove it, we iterate and look at a different hypothesis, such as "We should open new locations in South America." The clearer the hypothesis, the easier it is to prove or disprove it.

How to Create a Hypothesis

The process of creating a hypothesis is straightforward. Begin by referring to the question you generated in the first step. Either by yourself or in a team, come up with a meaningful number of possible answers for how you could answer the question. This idea-generation exercise can be as simple as writing down the first four or five ideas you have or as complex as a large, structured brainstorming session. At this stage, you will *not* assess the ideas beyond cursory sizing efforts or discussion of each idea's basic pros and cons.

Once you've generated your idea list, you have to make a difficult decision. You need to pick *one* of those ideas to be your initial hypothesis. This could be uncomfortable to do, especially if you're used to doing exhaustive analysis on *all* ideas before you select the best idea. To overcome this discomfort, shift your thinking from a parallel problem-solving process to a serial one. For example, in a parallel process, you'd conduct deep analysis on five ideas. Assuming each idea requires ten hours of analysis, that amounts to fifty hours of work before you're able to select the best idea from the set. The upside is you'll have certainty around which idea creates the most value. The downside is it takes you fifty hours to figure that out. Along the way you've analyzed one or two ideas that were low value. In the serial structured thought process, look at your list of five possible ideas and select the one you *feel* is most likely the best one. You'll conduct your ten hours of analysis on that one idea. You might get two hours into your analysis and determine your recommendation is a bad idea. When this happens, kill that idea and move on to the next most likely one on your list. After ten hours of analyzing idea #2, you find it has merit and take it forward as a recommendation. That's twelve hours of analysis to get to an answer versus fifty hours. In the worst case, if you're wrong with every one of your guesses, it would still take you fifty hours to analyze all five ideas in a serial sequence versus a parallel one. You're no worse off using the structured thought process than you would be doing your analysis the old way.

I can already hear someone screaming, "How can you *feel* which one is best without doing any analysis? How do you know idea #2 is the *best* idea?" Those are valid concerns. First, remember this is an iterative process. Many choices you make early in the structured thought process will change based upon analysis and input from others. This means your first choice of idea to analyze might not play out as being correct. That said, the process will eventually get you to the right answer. With that in mind, selecting a best guess as your initial hypothesis isn't complicated. Ask yourself a few questions to make the choice:

- ✑ Which idea looks like it's the largest opportunity?
- ✑ Which idea is most consistent with our strategy or organizational goals?
- ✑ Which idea will our stakeholder be most supportive of?
- ✑ Which idea has the highest likelihood of successful implementation?

These questions should lead you to a reasonable selection as your analytical starting point. If you're still having trouble selecting one of the options to begin with, you can conduct *simple* analysis to make a selection. Beware of getting sucked into deep analysis though. That defeats the purpose of being hypothesis driven.

The structured thought process operates under the premise that you can pursue one idea, and after you've completed it, you can move on to the second best idea on your list. That means you could end up finding a *good* idea with your first hypothesis and then find a *great* idea with your second hypothesis. Many leaders are supportive of that approach. They'd rather have an action-oriented team that captures value quickly versus an overly analytical team that does nothing but analysis in search of the optimal answer. The action-oriented team has been successful because they've generated value, even if they don't get the greatest value on their first attempt. Remember, while you're doing analysis, you're not generating value.

There will be scenarios where you have limited resources and you'll only get to pursue one idea. Those situations require you to try to find the best idea of all your options. This doesn't mean you do the full ten hours of analysis on every idea though. Instead, prioritize your ideas using the above questions, then conduct your analysis on the subset of most likely ideas. In this example, you may have five ideas. Don't do fifty hours of analysis. Pick your top three ideas and do thirty hours of analysis. Document why you thought the bottom two ideas lacked merit and move on. At any point in your analysis of the top three ideas, be open to killing the idea as soon as you have enough information to indicate it's not the best choice.

Once you've narrowed your idea list down to your best idea, you're ready to advance that hypothesis through the structured thought process. Be sure to document your initial thoughts on why you chose this hypothesis. Write down your rationale for not selecting the other ideas on your list. If you disprove your first hypothesis, you'll need to go back to your idea list and select your next best idea to take through the process. For now, settle on that single best idea and make it your preliminary recommendation.

4

Generate a *Core Idea*

At the heart of getting your pitch approved is making your audience care about it. The best way to make them care is to explain how your idea advances their agenda. Show them how your recommendation drives a result they're interested in. The way you make this linkage is through the creation of the core idea.

A core idea is sometimes referred to as an "elevator pitch." The reason it's called an "elevator pitch" is because you have approximately thirty seconds to deliver your message. That's the amount of time you'd be on the elevator with the stakeholder going from one floor to another. Imagine you get on an elevator and a senior stakeholder boards your elevator on the next floor. They proceed to ask you what you're working on. You can either ramble on about all the data you're gathering and the analysis you're doing, or you can give them a brief yet powerful explanation of the idea you're pursuing and why it's exciting. Ideally, the reason it's exciting is related to a metric or objective that stakeholder cares about. The latter approach is obviously preferable. By the time you finish your elevator ride together, the stakeholder knows what you're working on, and they're supportive of you pursuing the idea.

A core idea is composed of two elements. The first half entails you explaining the "what we should do" part of your recommendation. The second half is the "why we should do it" part of your pitch. At this stage you've already generated your "what we should do"; it's your hypothesis from the previous step. The "why we should do it" component depends upon your stakeholder. I refer to this component as the "button"—that metric or objective that makes your stakeholder sit up and take notice. Recall the earlier hypothesis about expanding into Italy and Germany. Let's turn that hypothesis into a core idea. I've listed a few stakeholders and corresponding core ideas to pitch to them regarding the European market entry:

Vice President of Sales: "We should enter the Italian and German markets because we can generate $XMM in sales."

Chief Financial Officer: "We should enter the Italian and German markets because we can generate $XMM in incremental profits."

Chief Marketing Officer: "We should enter the Italian and German markets because we can increase our European market share by X%."

Vice President of Human Resources: "We should enter the Italian and German markets because we can get access to a large, diverse talent pool."

Notice the hypothesis is the same every time. I'm making a pitch for entering the Italian and German markets no matter who my stakeholder is. But the button changes depending upon who I'm trying to influence. The VP of sales will care about sales. The CFO will care about profits. The CMO will care about market share. The VP of human resources will care about talent. I'm not pitching a one size fits all core idea. I'm tailoring it based upon who I'm trying to influence. The odds of me getting their support go up when I target my communications this way. Imagine if I pitched the same core idea to all those stakeholders: "We should enter the Italian and German markets because we can generate $19MM to $23MM in sales." The VP of sales would be excited because the idea drives sales. The CFO might be interested but would wonder how profitable those sales will be. The CMO would ask how much of a market share increase those sales translate to and wouldn't approve the idea until she had that answer. The VP of human resources might feel frustrated because I didn't explain the idea's talent implications. That core idea would get some support from this crowd but it wouldn't be unanimous and I would have questions I'd still need to answer.

Build a *Core Idea*: Hypothesis + Button

A good core idea combines an easily understood hypothesis with a button relevant to the stakeholder. First, get clear on your hypothesis. When you write down this part of your core idea, be specific and tell your audience what you want them to do. Beware of buzzwords that can be interpreted multiple ways. The worst and most prevalent buzzword out there is "leverage," as in "We should leverage our IT system." While that may sound great, the way the recommendation is phrased leaves room for confusion. One person might think it means we'll use our IT system in a full rollout of the initiative. Someone else might think we're running a pilot. Yet another might believe we'll let other companies use our IT system too so we can run more volume through that fixed asset. The point is, the word "leverage" leaves room for interpretation. That can cause confusion, which hampers your efforts to get your idea approved. Write the hypothesis portion of your core idea in simple yet precise language. If you say, "We should pilot a test of the new marketing model on our IT system," your core idea is more likely to be understood by everyone in the room—more so than "leverage our IT system." If stakeholders understand your recommendation, they'll know what you're asking them to approve.

The second component of the core idea is the button. The button is the one metric or objective that your stakeholder cares about more than any other. Sometimes the button is obvious: the VP of sales would like to drive sales. For other stakeholders, the button might not be self-evident. In those situations you have a few choices for how to figure out the stakeholder's button. You can get a copy of their goals or strategic plan. The metric they emphasize the most in those documents is their button. You can ask a member of their team what the stakeholder cares most about. You can ask the stakeholder what their objective is. If you can't access any of those sources, think through which metric matters the most to them and start with that. Remember, this is an iterative process. It's okay to get the button wrong on your first guess. As you iterate through the structured thought process, you'll get that piece of information. For now, put something on paper to advance through the process. Accept that it's a draft of your recommendation that will change as you learn more.

Once you've settled on a metric to use for the button, quantify it if possible. During these early stages, you may only have a rough value estimate. In many cases you won't have an estimate at all. For now include whatever you have as a placeholder that will be refined later. In the examples I provided earlier I wrote "$XMM" or "X%" to serve as a placeholder. That's acceptable—and encouraged—at this stage. The placeholder will serve as a reminder in future steps that you'll need to do the analysis to solve for X. If you use this approach, think through X's unit of measure. This process is about making it easy for your stakeholder to say yes to your pitch. If they think in percentages and you give them "$X," you're asking them to do math. The same holds true if they think in dollars and you give them "X%." These extra steps aren't required if you do the math for them. Small points like this may not seem to matter, but these are the details that differentiate a rough pitch from an elegant one. Elegance is about simplicity and smoothness. These small changes are ways you can smooth the rough spots in your pitch.

Stakeholders are not one-dimensional. They have several buttons they care about. You may be tempted to push multiple buttons in your core idea. If one button is good, then two is better, therefore ten would be awesome! Right? Wrong. Adding buttons has a dilutive effect. The structured thought process is about simplicity. Focus on the most important buttons. The maximum number of buttons I recommend including in a core idea is three. Having more than three buttons gets confusing. Witness the following examples:

"We should enter the Italian and German markets because we can generate $XMM in sales, $YMM in profits, and increase market share by Z%."

Versus:

"We should enter the Italian and German markets because we can generate $XMM in sales, $YMM in profits, increase market share by Z%, improve customer satisfaction by D%, reduce costs by $EMM, increase morale by F%, and increase system availability by G%."

The first example is manageable. The second one gets downright overwhelming! It becomes a long and painful elevator ride, doesn't it? Limit yourself to three buttons at the most.

Address Multiple Stakeholders Simultaneously

There will be situations where you'll need to pitch your idea to multiple stakeholders at the same time. Each stakeholder might have a different button. If you have fifteen stakeholders in the room, including all their buttons can make for a long core idea. This situation requires you to prioritize your efforts and manage the conversation.

First, determine who is deciding versus who is participating. Focus your core idea on the decision makers. Don't tailor your core idea to stakeholders who are only sitting in on the session. Their ability to affect your pitch's outcome isn't as large as your decision makers' ability to do so. Once you've identified the decision makers, select your buttons accordingly. When you write your core idea, prioritize the sequence of your buttons. To prioritize, determine which button will appeal the most to the decision makers. If several stakeholders are financially focused and one is concerned with system uptime, cover the financial button first and the uptime button second. If I'm presenting predominantly to stakeholders with financial interests and a few stakeholders with uptime interests, my core idea could be: "We should enter the Italian and German markets because we can generate $YMM in profits and increase system availability by G%." Conversely, if my CIO is the primary decision maker and there are a few more junior finance decision makers in the room, my core idea would be "We should enter the Italian and German markets because we can increase system availability by G% and generate $YMM in profits." The most important button goes first. Importance is determined by your audience.

Don't obsess about wordsmithing or perfecting your core idea at this stage. As you move through the process, the core idea will evolve. The stakeholders you're presenting to could change. For now, be thoughtful about generating a clear hypothesis and include buttons that will appeal to your expected stakeholders. Include placeholders like "X" as a reminder to do that analysis in future steps.

Your Audience Comes First

People have a natural tendency to create their pitch from their own perspective. When they do, they include a button that's relevant to them but may not resonate with their audience. The result is predictable: a lack of audience support for the idea. Personally, I've made this mistake on several occasions, looking at the core idea from my perspective versus that of my audience. Those pitches didn't go well.

One pitch in particular stands out, and I'll never forget it. I was trying to land a partnership with an important company. The deal would have helped my company grow substantially. I was fortunate enough to get an audience with the senior decision maker at the partner company. I spent several hours preparing for the meeting by honing my pitch until I thought it was perfect. Despite my outward confidence, I was a nervous wreck going into the meeting. This had the potential to be a huge deal for me.

The partner company's decision maker listened while I made my pitch. When I finished, I expected to hear "Great! I love it. Let's move forward with the partnership." Instead, I was greeted with a pointed question: "So what's in it for me?" That's a terrifying question to field in the moment you realize you haven't thought about your pitch from your audience's perspective. Everything in my pitch talked about why this was a great idea for *me and my company*. There was nothing in the pitch that spelled out the tremendous benefits for the prospective partner company. I didn't close the deal that day. I didn't even come close.

Luckily, I was granted a second opportunity to pitch my idea to this decision maker. I reflected on my failed first pitch and approached the second one from the stake-holder's perspective. The recommendation was still the same, that we should form a partnership. But this time I made sure the decision maker came first. I articulated all the benefits they would receive from partnering with me. That meeting was a rousing success, and I was able to close the deal. Even though the recommendation was the same, I got a different outcome the second time around because I put my audience's needs first.

Finalize Your *Core Idea*

Once you have an actionable hypothesis and a clear sense of your audience's buttons, write down your core idea. Documenting the end products from each step of the structured thought process is part of the discipline of applying this approach. You'll need this core idea to conduct future steps of the process. Writing it down lets your core idea serve as a reference to build upon. Writing forces you to be more precise in the language you use. When we speak, we tend to use far more words to explain something than when we write down the same idea. The clearer your core idea is, the easier it will be for your audience to understand it. That written core idea will make building your architecture a straightforward process.

When writing your core idea, be sure to follow the sequence of hypothesis, then button. Many times I see people put the button first, then address their hypothesis. The reason they do this is they think they'll get the stakeholder's attention by putting the button first. If I came to you and said, "We can save $2MM by...," I would get your attention. But this approach carries risks with it. While my intent is to focus you on the next words out of my mouth—which will be my hypothesis—putting the button first could lead you to do anything but focus on my idea. As soon as I say "$2MM" your brain will come up with an idea for where I plan on capturing those savings. The problem is your idea is not the same idea I'm about to recommend. I then have a challenge: I'll need to move you off your idea and onto mine. That effort expended getting you to drop your idea is wasteful.

For this example, let's assume my core idea is: "We should consolidate our supplier base and use volume purchasing for office supplies because we can save $2MM per year." If I put the button first and say, "We can save $2MM," you might fill in that blank with "by laying off people on the headquarters staff." The next thing you know, we're talking about who to fire and how we'll reorganize staff. By putting the button first, I've lost control of the conversation. I've seen an entire meeting get derailed because the presenter said the button before they offered their hypothesis. The result was we had to have another meeting to talk about the recommendation because we spent all our time in the first meeting discussing a different idea. It was a poor use of everyone's time.

When you put the hypothesis first and then share the button, you're leading your audience in a more natural sequence. People tend to think in terms of cause and effect. The hypothesis is the cause and the button is the effect. If I present you a core idea that starts with "We should consolidate our supplier base and use volume purchasing for office supplies, " there's one natural question that comes to mind: Why? I've given you the cause, and now you want to know the effect. I have your attention, and I'm leading you to my conclusion versus one you create on your own. I can then tell you "because we can save \$2MM per year." If you're excited by the button of \$2MM—which you should be if I've done my homework—your next likely question is: How can we do that? That becomes my cue to take you deeper into my pitch, which is what I want to happen. A core idea that follows the sequence of hypothesis then button will lead your audience to first be interested in your idea and second to want to know more about it.

After you've written down your core idea, check it for quality. Ask yourself the following questions:

- Is my recommendation (hypothesis) clear and actionable?
- Will people unfamiliar with this idea know what I'm recommending they do?
- Do I have a button that will resonate with my stakeholder?
- Have I written my core idea in the correct sequence of hypothesis first and button second?
- Do I have a placeholder for the value my idea will generate (e.g., \$XMM, X%)?
- If I'm pushing multiple buttons, do I have no more than three?
- Have I sequenced my buttons in order of importance to my stakeholder?

Once you're satisfied with your core idea and can answer the questions above in the affirmative, you're ready to start building your support for your recommendation.

5

Architecture *Benefits* and Approaches

Before we explore architecture, I'd like you to participate in a little exercise. Spend two minutes to take the ideas below and arrange them into logical groups. Those are the only instructions I'll provide. Go!

Ace	Falcons
Colts	Birdie
Chip	Pocket
Albatross	Eagle
Wild Card	Lions
Broncos	Rake
Quarter	Club

After you got past your initial reaction of wondering how many groups to create and realizing you could place the same idea in different groups, you likely settled on one of two common groupings. One pairing is golf and American football:

Golf	American Football
Ace (a hole in one)	Wild Card (a playoff spot)
Birdie (one shot under par)	Quarter (one of four timed periods in a football game)
Eagle (two shots under par)	Pocket (where the quarterback stays when he prepares to throw a pass)
Albatross (hole in one on a par four)	Falcons (Atlanta Falcons)
Club (golf club)	Broncos (Denver Broncos)
Chip (a short shot near the green)	Colts (Indianapolis Colts)
Rake (to smooth a sand trap after walking in it)	Lions (Detroit Lions)

A second pairing is poker and animals:

Poker	Animals
Ace (the highest card in a suit)	Lions (kings of the jungle)
Quarter (twenty-five cents, a common betting denomination)	Birdie (a small, winged creature with feathers)
Pocket (the two facedown cards a player receives when playing Texas Hold 'Em)	Albatross (a big, ugly sea bird)
Wild Card (a playing card that can play the role of any card the player desires)	Falcons (raptors that hunt small animals)
Club (one of four suits in a deck of cards)	Broncos (untrained horses)
Chip (a token used for betting)	Colts (young horses)
Rake (to take the pot when a player wins a poker hand)	Eagle (a large raptor that typically symbolizes freedom)

If you're not familiar with golf and American football and you didn't get those groups, you could have arrived at groupings of:

long words and short words

monosyllabic and polysyllabic

begins with a vowel and begins with a consonant

even number of letters and odd number of letters

The point is, there are many ways to arrange the same information. The way we arrange it is based on *our* perspective. If you're an avid golfer who loves to watch the National Football League on a Sunday, you likely jumped straight to golf and football. If you enjoy playing cards with your friends and going to the zoo, you probably arrived at poker and animals. I've given this exercise to many people. Sometimes they'll accuse me of being male-centric or Americentric. Those accusations are unfair. All I've done is offer a list of words. I haven't offered any interpretation of them. While golf and football or poker and animals do lean toward being Americentric male groupings, nothing about the exercise itself is. If you happen to be a non-American female and if none of those words were familiar, you could still do the exercise and get a result that satisfies the objective of placing the ideas into logical groups as demonstrated above. All I did in this exercise was present you with raw, unstructured data. I gave you chaos, and chaos is uncomfortable. We have an innate desire to put order to chaos. The way we create that order is by arranging information according to how *we* perceive it.

Our perception is shaped by our beliefs and experiences. Here's where perceptions get problematic when you're trying to communicate: If I'm coming to pitch you an idea that's related to poker and animals but I give you unstructured chaos, I run the risk of you arranging that information into groups of golf and football. I now have two challenges. First, I have to get you to stop thinking about golf and football—which is hard because it's the construct you came up with. Second, I have to get you thinking about poker and animals. By the time I get you looking at the information through the lens I want you to view it through, the meeting is over. Failure to structure information leads to misunderstandings.

What if my instructions for this exercise were instead to arrange these ideas into groups of poker and animals, and then I presented the data to you? What's the likelihood you would have arrived at my groupings in the poker and animals solution? The odds are good you'll arrive at the solution I want you to arrive at. Even if you don't know all the poker terms you could still arrive at my answer by using a logical process of elimination. Providing people with structure before providing them information gets them to see the facts through the lens you want them to look through. That lens is your recommendation's architecture.

Architecture Provides *Structure*

Architecture is the arrangement of thoughts and ideas into logical groups with the intent of influencing your audience to arrive at your conclusion. The conclusion you're working toward is the core idea. Building an architecture is the most difficult step of the structured thought process. It's also the most critical one. Architecture goes beyond grouping ideas. Your architecture will show the linkages between ideas, how those ideas relate to the core idea, and provide a means for pressure testing your argument's strength.

If you build a solid architecture, the rest of the process is easy. The architecture shows you how to craft your story, guides you toward the right analyses, and enables you to draft a communication that's clear, concise, and compelling. You'll sequence your final communication based upon the architecture you create in this step. If you don't invest effort in creating your architecture, you risk performing unnecessary analysis, gathering irrelevant information, and delivering a final communication that's unclear at best and confusing at worst.

As you're applying the structured thought process, you should hear warning sirens go off if you find yourself saying "I don't have time to create an architecture. I'm going to skip ahead to analysis." Skipping ahead will indeed get you working on analysis sooner; however, it might be the *wrong* analysis. Without an architecture, you might miss performing an analysis which could lead your entire argument to crumble. You would then need to go back and try proving your case again. That approach is inefficient. It takes more time than doing it right the first time. This step is the key to being more efficient with how you spend your time. Architecture eliminates wasted work.

Architecture doesn't only make you more efficient by telling you which analyses to do and which analyses to avoid. It also makes your communications clearer and crisper. You'll find your presentation's length drops from twenty to forty pages down to ten to fifteen. Your memos will no longer spill over to multiple pages. Your emails won't require the reader to scroll down several times to read your entire message. Instead, they will be read and understood on the first pass. Architecture can help you leave clearer voicemails that are responded to versus deleted because they ramble. If you write business cases, architecture will make your idea's benefits apparent, thereby increasing the chances your case is approved.

Creating an architecture is a visual effort. Find a whiteboard, markers, and an eraser. I suggest using a whiteboard instead of scratch paper or a flip chart. As you create your architecture, you'll change it several times. It's better to make those changes on a whiteboard because your architecture will be easier to read than if you create it on a flip chart and have ideas scratched out all over the place. Ideally, you'll be able to find a whiteboard where you can leave your architecture up for a while. As you progress through the structured thought process, you'll refer back to your architecture often, modify it as you learn new information, and use it to create the outputs of future process steps.

Choosing an *Architecture* Approach

While there's an infinite array of architectures you can build, there are two primary structures you'll use to build them. These basic building blocks are the layer approach and the column approach. You'll choose your architecture based upon your audience's familiarity with your topic as well as their level of support or resistance for your idea. When you draw your architecture, always have the core idea at the top of the picture because that's what you're supporting with all the information below it. Placing the core idea at the top shows you how to construct the rest of the architecture.

The Layer Approach

A layer approach starts with background on your topic for the purpose of grounding everyone. It then moves to a change that has happened which is leading you to make a recommendation. That's then topped off with your core idea. The layer architecture graphic on the next page, Figure 5.1, explains what to include in each layer.

Core Idea
This is the core idea created in the prior step of the structured thought process.

What's Changed?
- This is what's leading you to look at this issue and make a recommendation for change (your core idea).
- This can be an event, a change in time period, new information, or some combination of those three things.
- This can be something negative that is forcing action or something positive that's creating a new opportunity.

Background
- Include background the audience isn't familiar with.
- Provide information that must be understood for the "What's Changed?" section to make sense.
- Make sure the information provided isn't controversial, if possible.

Figure 5.1

The layer approach should be selected in two situations:

Situation #1: The audience lacks context. When your audience is unfamiliar with your subject matter, a layer approach is an appropriate choice. The architecture's "Background" portion ensures everyone is operating from the same basis of fact. Without that background, your audience won't understand the context surrounding your core idea and therefore can't be supportive of it.

Situation #2: The audience is resistant. Your audience may have context related to your core idea but they don't *like* your core idea. A layer approach can bring a resistant audience along from their place of resistance to a place where they're at least open to listening to your idea. The "What's Changed" layer creates the case for action that should inspire your audience to approve your core idea.

The Column Approach

The column approach starts with the core idea, and below it are columns of information supporting it. That information will be broken up into categories like the grouping exercise you did in the Poker/Animals exercise. The number of columns will be a function of what you've included in your core idea. The architecture will typically include two to five columns total. Figure 5.2 on the next page shows what a column architecture can look like.

Core Idea This is the core idea created in the prior step of the structured thought process.		
Column 1	Column 2	Column 3
• This column covers one topic area required to prove your core idea. • All facts within this colunn are related to the subject matter of the column itself.	• This column covers one topic area required to prove your core idea. • All facts within this column are related to the subject matter of the column itself.	• This column covers one topic area required to prove your core idea. • All facts within this column are related to the subject matter of the column itself.

Figure 5.2

The column approach should be selected in situations where your audience is familiar with the subject matter and doesn't require all the context you would provide in a layer approach. You'll often find your direct manager and stakeholders you interact with frequently will be appropriate audiences for a column approach.

Select an *Architecture* Approach

Sometimes your choice of architecture is easy. You may know you're pitching your idea to an uninformed audience, which leads you to a layer approach. You could be taking your idea to your boss who is well versed in the subject matter, so a column approach is a natural choice. But there will be times you won't be sure which approach to use. You might not know how familiar your audience is with the subject matter. Their level of support or resistance for your idea could be a mystery. You may be faced with a situation where you're pitching to multiple stakeholders in the same meeting and some require a column approach but others would be more receptive to a layer approach. Architecture choice can be a complex exercise.

To simplify your architecture choice, segment your audience and remain flexible. If you're not sure if the audience needs a column or a layer, start with a layer. As you progress through the "Background" and "What's Changed" sections, be attuned to their reactions. If they're listening and moving at your pace, a layer was an appropriate choice. If they appear impatient and ask questions like "I already know this. Why are you covering this again?" be prepared to shift to your core idea and any columns you've built to support it.

If you have a mixed audience where some need a column and others need a layer, prioritize your efforts. Build your architecture in a way that focuses on the *key* decision makers in the meeting. If ten people in the meeting need a layer but your two primary decision makers require a column, go with a column. While using a column approach will require you to get the other ten people the background prior to the meeting, your pitch will go more smoothly with your audience members.

Conversely, if the key people you're trying to influence require a layer but everyone else in the room would prefer a column, go with a layer. While this could frustrate those in the room who have context, you'll never get approval if your main decision makers aren't walked through the entire layer approach. To minimize this frustration, tell those column audience members you acknowledge their familiarity with the subject but you're going through the "Background" and "What's Changed" sections so everyone in the room is making a decision from a place of common understanding. By acknowledging their understanding of the context, you reduce their frustration with having to go over it again. They'll understand getting the decision makers up to speed is in the interest of making a good decision.

Over time, you'll find architecture approaches that will be comfortable for you. That doesn't matter. What matters is what's comfortable for your *audience*. The more you pitch ideas to stakeholders using the structured thought process, the easier it will be to select the correct architecture for that situation. Always assess the audience and the subject matter. While you may use a column approach with a particular stakeholder in one meeting, you might require a layer approach for the same stakeholder for a different pitch. This will occur because the stakeholder was familiar with the first idea but unfamiliar with the second one. The choice of architecture approach is an important one. Invest the time thinking through which approach you'll use and why you're choosing to use it. That extra time you spend up front will make the final pitch go more smoothly in the end.

Build an *Architecture*

Building your architecture is the heart of the structured thought process. Fortunately, it's a simple concept. Unfortunately, people tend to overcomplicate creating the architecture. Remember, the reason you're building an architecture is to prove your core idea in a manner that's understandable to your audience. When you build your architecture, you might have an urge to gather all the facts you know related to your core idea, then assemble them into your architecture. Don't do that! You'll end up with a logic jalopy comprising many different facts that lack a coherent structure to tie them all together. Instead, let your core idea and your audience drive your architecture's construction.

The first step in building your architecture is finding a whiteboard. Once you've secured your whiteboard space, draw a box at the top of the whiteboard. Write your core idea in that box. Don't shorten it or abbreviate anything. Write the *entire* core idea. Next, define your audience. If you're pitching your idea to multiple stakeholders, identify the primary stakeholder you're trying to influence. Write their name on the whiteboard next to your core idea. This will serve as a constant reminder of who you're focusing on for your architecture. Based upon that individual's understanding of the issue, determine if you'll use a layer approach or a column approach. You may find situations where you're combining the layer approach and column approach in a single architecture. I encourage those combinations if they help your audience understand your recommendation. I'll illustrate how this works as I build an example architecture in this chapter.

Once you have your core idea and your architecture approach selected, it's time to start drawing boxes. The easiest way to build your architecture is to build from the top down. Later in the process, we'll prove your core idea from the bottom up. To build from the top down, start by underlining major concepts in your core idea. For example, imagine we're pitching our idea to the CFO and our core idea is: "We should enter the Italian and German markets because we can generate $XMM in sales, $YMM in profits, and increase market share by Z%."

There are four major concepts we'll need to support:

We should enter the **Italian and German markets** *because we can generate* **$XMM in sales**, **$YMM in profits**, *and* **increase market share by Z%**.

The CFO has been in her role for a while. She knows the business well and is familiar with why we're looking at international expansion. In this situation, we could use a column approach for our architecture. By building from the top down, the core idea tells us we need four columns: "Enter new markets," "Increase sales," "Increase profits," and "Increase market share." Within each column we will include points of support related to that column. In the "Enter new markets" column, we might cover what it takes to enter Italy and what it takes to enter Germany. In the "Increase sales" column we could cover increasing sales in Italy and in Germany. In the "Increase profits" column we might discuss our profit margins in Italy, our margins in Germany, and the total profits we would generate in those combined markets. In the final column, "Increase market share," the supporting points could include our current market share in Italy, Germany, and Europe, as well as our future market share in those markets. Our preliminary architecture might look like Figure 6.1 on the next page.

Every component of the core idea has support somewhere in the architecture below. The points in each column relate to the subject matter of that column alone; all my sales points are in the sales column, all my profit points are in the profit column, and so on. While those points relate to points in another column (e.g., sales is related to market share) the bullets have a *direct* relationship to the column's subject matter.

You may be wondering where all the bullet points in the architecture came from. Like your core idea, those points are hypotheses at this stage of the structured

Core Idea

We should enter the <u>Italian and German markets</u> because we can generate <u>$XMM in sales</u>, <u>$YMM in profits</u>, and <u>increase market share by Z%</u>.

Enter New Markets	Increase Sales	Increase Profits	Increase Market Share
• Market entry requirements for entering Italy • Market entry requirements for entering Germany	• Sales totals expected in Italy ($AMM) • Sales totals expected in Germany ($BMM) • $AMM + $BMM = $XMM	Margins • Profit margin in Italy (C%) • Profit margin in Germany (D%) Total Profits • Total profits expected in Italy ($EMM) • Total profits expected in Germany ($FMM) • $EMM + $FMM = $YMM	Current • Current share in Italy (G%) • Current share in Germany (H%) • Current share in Europe (J%) Future • Share increase in Italy (K%) • Share increase in Germany (L%) • Share increase in Europe (K% + L% = Z%)

Figure 6.1

thought process. They're our best guess as to what pieces of information we could include to support our argument. As we move through the process and speak with people, gather data, and conduct analysis, we might find those bullet points change based upon new information. For now they serve as a good starting point for trying to prove our case. This is another reason I encourage the use of a whiteboard; these bullets might change when we get new information. In those situations, it's easy to erase or modify the bullet point on the whiteboard.

There are many ways to create an architecture. In this next example, imagine my audience is the business unit presidents for the Italian business unit and the German business unit. I'll be presenting to both of them at the same time. I would take a different approach to my architecture for this situation than I would with the CFO who has a more global perspective. Instead of four separate columns, I might create two columns and then have more detailed columns below them. The architecture could look like Figure 6.2 on the next page.

Core Idea

We should enter the Italian and German markets because we can generate $XMM in sales, $YMM in profits, and increase market share by Z%.

Enter Italian Market

- Enter Italy because it generates $AMM in sales and $BMM in profits, and increases market share C%.

Enter Italian Market	Increase sales in Italy	Increase profits in Italy	Increase share in Italy
• How to enter the Italian Market	• Sales totals expected in Italy ($AMM)	• Profit totals expected in Italy ($BMM)	• Market share expected in Italy (C%)

Enter German Market

- Enter Germany because it generates $DMM in sales and $EMM in profits, and increases market share F%.

Enter German Market	Increase sales in Germany	Increase profits in Germany	Increase share in Germany
• How to enter the German Market	• Sales totals expected in Germany ($DMM)	• Profit totals expected in Germany ($EMM)	• Market share expected in Germany (F%)

Figure 6.2

Most of the information is the same, but it's arranged differently. All my numbers would have to add up to my targets in the core idea. In this case, it breaks down like this:

- ∽ $AMM in Italian sales plus $DMM in German sales equals the $XMM in total sales in the core idea.

- ∽ $BMM in Italian profits plus $EMM in German profits equals the $YMM in total profits in the core idea.

- ∽ The C% Italian market share plus the F% German market share generates the Z% total market share increase cited in the core idea.

When you're drafting your architecture, these place-holder variables are reminders of future analyses you'll need to perform. I suggest using different letters for each variable to prevent confusion that could arise from double counting or talking about the wrong metric. It prevents you from getting caught up in a "*this* X%, not *that* X%!" conversation when you use the same letter for a different variable.

Let's look at why this architecture is different than the one we used with the CFO.

The audience for the first pitch is the CFO. She needs a global perspective and is interested in the total impact on corporate sales, profits, and market share. She's interested in what our resultant European market share would be after entering these two markets. Giving her a combined picture of sales, profits, and share from both markets enables her to focus on the three financial metrics she's most interested in. With this architecture, she won't have to go to two separate sections to find numbers and add them up for each metric.

The audience for the second pitch consists of two business unit leaders. The head of the Italian business has marginal interest in the German market. He'd prefer to see all the information related to his business in one section. He would find it uninteresting or even distracting to have German numbers intertwined with those for his Italian business. His German counterpart would want the same thing, to have her German business broken out from the Italian business.

In the second pitch, there's no mention of the combined market share for our European business. It's left out because neither the Italian business unit head nor the German business unit head care about total European market share. While that fact is important in the first architecture because the CFO wants to know total share, it's a distraction in the second situation.

In both examples, the architectures are column approaches. This architecture choice is appropriate because the audiences in both cases are grounded on the situation and don't require additional information to make a decision. In the second example, the first level of columns is the business unit: Italy is column 1 and Germany is column 2. The level below that is also a column approach because the Italian business unit head knows his business and doesn't need context. The same holds true for the German business unit head.

The audience drives the different choice of approaches for how to construct the architecture. While at this stage of the structured thought process no one is seeing your work, you do need to be mindful of how you'll structure the work you eventually share with your audience. Don't get hung up on making your architecture perfect. You'll have plenty of opportunities to refine it as you go through the process. For now, spend time thinking through what information your audience will need to support your pitch as well as the best way to structure how you'll share that information with that particular audience.

Combined Architecture Approaches

Some situations will require a hybrid approach to building your architecture. Your audience may be familiar with some components of your pitch but unfamiliar with others. To deal with those scenarios, apply the architecture approach selection rules for *each level* of your architecture. You can combine the layer approach and column approach to tailor your pitch to your audience's information needs.

Let's explore an example. In this case, imagine you work at a credit card company. You've never worked in the financial services industry before; all your prior roles were in the aviation industry. I've been assigned as a member of your team, and you're my primary stakeholder. I need to pitch you an idea to get you to invest in a new piece of technology. I've settled on this core idea: "We should buy a new dialer from Vendor ABC to reduce our losses by $XMM per year."

I know you're new to the industry and don't have context for making this decision. Given that, I've chosen a layer approach for making my pitch to you. I made that decision because you're not grounded on the situation. I need to ensure you understand the context of the

Core Idea
We should buy a new dialer from Vendor ABC to reduce our losses by $XMM per year.

What's Changed?
- The economy has been tough, and our losses have increased as a result.
- Our current dialer is old and keeps breaking down.
- We've learned Vendor ABC is selling a new dialer that will cut our losses.
- We estimate we can cut our losses by $XMM by using the new dialer.

Background
- In the credit card industry, we loan money to consumers based on how risky they are.
- Consumers don't always pay us back, and when they don't, we experience losses.
- When they don't pay us back, we pursue collections activities using a piece of technology called a dialer.
- The dialer determines whom to call on the phone, when to call, and how often to call, as we try to collect our money.

Figure 6.3

recommendation before I make my pitch. A layer approach is the most effective way to do that. When you read the following layer architecture, read the "Background" section first, then "What's Changed," and then the core idea. It will make more sense that way. My initial architecture looks like Figure 6.3 to the left.

In the "Background" section, I ground you and provide context about how our business works, how our customers behave, and how we collect money when customers don't pay us back. Then I move to creating a case for action in the "What's Changed" layer by pointing out two major negative changes we've experienced. Increasing losses and old technology are causing issues for our business and we need to take action. I've included new information about Vendor ABC's dialer and how it could impact our business. Given that background and those changes, my recommendation to replace the dialer makes sense and appears to be a good idea.

If I'm able to get your approval, I know the next audience I need to pitch is the VP of collections. He's worked in the collections industry for fifteen years. If I go to him with a layer approach, he'll throw me out of his office! Can you imagine his reaction if I begin my pitch by explaining how we make risk-based lending decisions to consumers and how dialers work? He already knows all that information because of his deep industry expertise. He'll need a column approach instead. My architecture for pitching him could look like this:

Core Idea		
We should buy a new dialer from Vendor ABC to reduce our losses by $XMM per year.		
Buy a New Dialer	Buy from Vendor ABC	Reduce Losses
• Our dialer is old and keeps breaking down. • There are newer and better dialers on the market. • A better, more reliable dialer will improve our collections performance.	• Vendor ABC sells high-quality dialers. • Vendor ABC has competitive pricing. • Only one other vendor's products (Vendor DEF) are approved by our IT group. • Vendor DEF's product is inferior to Vendor ABC's.	• Our losses have increased by $ZMM this year. • A new dialer could deliver loss reduction of $XMM per year.

Figure 6.4

All elements of my core idea are supported somewhere within the architecture. Each major concept in the core idea has support for it in both architectures: "We should **buy a new dialer** from **vendor ABC** to **reduce our losses by $XMM** per year."

In the layer approach, I discuss the dialer in the "Background" and in the "What's Changed" sections. I discuss Vendor ABC in the "What's Changed" section. I explain losses in the "Background" and "What's Changed" sections. In the column approach, each column is designed to support each of the major concepts in the core idea. When I pitch this idea to my VP of collections, I'll explain my core idea, then offer my three columns of information as support for the recommendation. The architecture is tailored to his information needs.

Once I get our VP of collections on board, there are two more stakeholders I'll need to convince—the CIO and the CFO. They both have a basic knowledge of dialers and how collections works. They don't need grounding on our business, how we make lending decisions, and how we get our money back. A column approach will be most appropriate for them. I know both of them are detail-oriented executives, and they'll expect me to come with another level of support to make my case. This situation calls for me to combine layer and column approaches. When I go pitch to the CIO, I would use an architecture that looks like Figure 6.5 on the next page.

Figure 6.5

Core Idea

We should buy a new dialer from Vendor ABC to reduce our losses by $XMM per year.

Buy a New Dialer
- Our current dialer doesn't work well.
- A new dialer will work better.

Current dialer issues
- Dialer was bought ten years ago.
- Software is outdated.
- Spare parts are hard to come by.
- It lacks critical features.

Future dialer capabilities
- Most modern software and calling models.
- 24/7 support is available.
- Likely to have all our must-have features and many nice-to-have ones.

Buy From Vendor ABC
- Vendor ABC has a more competitive product.
- Vendor DEF doesn't meet our needs.

Vendor ABC capabilities
- Vendor ABC sells high-quality dialers.
- Vendor ABC has competitive pricing.
- Vendor ABC is approved by our IT group.

Vendor DEF capabilities
- Vendor DEF's product is inferior to Vendor ABC's.
- Vendor DEF's pricing is 20% higher than Vendor ABC's.
- Vendor DEF is approved by our IT group.

Reduce Losses
- A new dialer could deliver loss reduction of $XMM per year.

What's Changed? Increasing losses
- Our losses have increased by $ZMM this year.
- Our current dialer is unable to keep up with increasing losses.
- New dialers are more effective at trimming losses.

Background: Collections losses
- Losses over the last five years have remained consistent at $YMM/year.
- In the past, our current dialers could manage those losses.

For the technology-related columns about the dialer and the technology vendors, I selected a column approach to support the main column. The CIO is familiar enough with the dialers and the vendors that a column approach will be an appropriate way to share that information. He's less familiar with the dialer's impact on losses and what our loss history looks like. For that column, I chose a layer approach. First, I ground the CIO on our past loss history, then I explain how our losses have changed in recent years. With that context, the loss reduction we expect from installing a new dialer makes sense.

When I go to take the same recommendation to the CFO, I need to construct a different architecture that's tailored to her information needs. I would create an architecture that looks like Figure 6.6 on the next page.

Figure 6.6

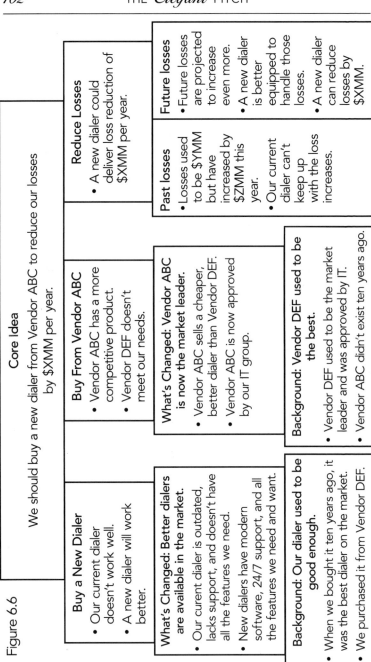

Core Idea
We should buy a new dialer from Vendor ABC to reduce our losses by $XMM per year.

Buy a New Dialer
- Our current dialer doesn't work well.
- A new dialer will work better.

What's Changed: Better dialers are available in the market.
- Our current dialer is outdated, lacks support, and doesn't have all the features we need.
- New dialers have modern software, 24/7 support, and all the features we need and want.

Background: Our dialer used to be good enough.
- When we bought it ten years ago, it was the best dialer on the market.
- We purchased it from Vendor DEF.

Buy From Vendor ABC
- Vendor ABC has a more competitive product.
- Vendor DEF doesn't meet our needs.

What's Changed: Vendor ABC is now the market leader.
- Vendor ABC sells a cheaper, better dialer than Vendor DEF.
- Vendor ABC is now approved by our IT group.

Background: Vendor DEF used to be the best.
- Vendor DEF used to be the market leader and was approved by IT.
- Vendor ABC didn't exist ten years ago.

Reduce Losses
- A new dialer could deliver loss reduction of $XMM per year.

Past losses
- Losses used to be $YMM but have increased by $ZMM this year.
- Our current dialer can't keep up with the loss increases.

Future losses
- Future losses are projected to increase even more.
- A new dialer is better equipped to handle those losses.
- A new dialer can reduce losses by $XMM.

For the first two technology-based columns, I selected a layer approach because the CFO is unfamiliar with the dialer or the technology vendors. She needs more context, therefore a layer approach is appropriate. The CFO does understand losses, which makes a column approach a better architecture choice for the third major column. In both of these examples my audience drives my architecture choice at *all levels* because each stakeholder has different levels of understanding. By targeting my architecture to their knowledge or lack thereof, I improve the likelihood that they'll understand my pitch.

Multiple Architechtures for *Multiple* Audiences

Different audiences need different architectures. This concept has large implications. It means you'll need to construct *multiple* architectures when you have multiple stakeholders. This may sound like extra work, but it will save you time in the long run. When you build a one-size-fits-all architecture and share it with multiple stakeholders who all have differing informational needs, it becomes a one-size-fits-none architecture. Stakeholders will understand portions of it but get lost in others. While the layer approach you create for one section of your architecture makes perfect sense to one stakeholder, another stakeholder will be frustrated by it. Your column approach in another section will be clear to one stakeholder and baffling to another. In your attempt to be efficient by building a single architecture, you've made your pitches that follow less efficient. You'll find yourself holding meetings two and three times to explain your pitch because it's based on a confusing architecture. You'll lose credibility because people won't understand what you're talking about.

When you tailor your architecture to each audience you're pitching to, you increase the likelihood of them understanding and approving your pitch on their first time through the material. As you continue through the structured thought process, you'll see the architecture will define the analysis you perform and how you construct your final presentation or memo. If your architecture is built with a specific audience in mind, you'll end up bringing the right information to the meeting, leaving the distracting information behind, and you'll have a productive conversation with that stakeholder. The result of tailoring your architecture to your audience is a series of shorter meetings that focus on giving each audience the information they need to make a decision. That leads to getting your pitch approved in the first meeting rather than having multiple confusing meetings based on a one-size-fits-none architecture.

There will be many situations where you have multiple stakeholders in the same meeting and each stakeholder requires a different architecture. That's a challenging meeting. The approach I recommend is to identify the *key* stakeholder and target your architecture toward their needs. This stakeholder is the person with final decision authority or the most influential person in the room. Their support or opposition to your pitch can sway the entire outcome. Focus on building your architecture to meet their needs for that particular meeting. This will require you to handle the other stakeholders accordingly. If your key stakeholder needs a column approach but everyone else needs a layer approach, construct both and try to get the background information to your layer-oriented audience members before the meeting. Let them know you won't be covering the background or what's changed in the meeting because the key stakeholder already has that context. Conversely, if your key stakeholder needs a layer approach and everyone else in the room needs a column approach, you can tell those stakeholders you're going to cover the background and what's changed for the sake of your key stakeholder before moving on to the information they're most interested in. Acknowledge their knowledge of the topic and ask them to be patient as you get others caught up to a similar level of understanding.

This approach of using different architectures for different audiences isn't a new concept. Think of this as marketing an idea. Marketers create different messages focused on different market segments. Your stakeholders are those different segments, therefore they require different messages. You're selling an idea the same way a marketer sells a product. Craft your architecture with an eye toward getting your stakeholder to buy your idea. Investing time in thinking about this during your pitch's early stages will save you time in the latter stages when your stakeholders support your idea the first time they hear it.

Once you've completed the first draft of your architecture, test its quality. There are two characteristics to evaluate: your thoughts need to be both distinct and complete. Fancy management consultants refer to this as being "MECE," which stands for "mutually exclusive and collectively exhaustive." A simpler description is no gaps and no overlaps. Regardless of how you describe these quality considerations, you need to apply them. If your architecture elements are distinct and complete, your architecture will be easier to understand and remember. It will be stronger because you won't be missing any information required to make your case.

Stress Test Your Architecture: Be *Distinct*

The ideas in one column or one layer must be separate, or distinct, from the ideas in another column or layer. For example, in our prior architecture about the German market and the Italian market, those concepts are distinct. There's a clear boundary to the information contained in those columns. The same holds true in the poker/animals example; each word in that exercise only belongs in one of those groupings. If instead of using the German market and the Italian market I used the columns "Western Europe" and "Southern Europe," my architecture would be confusing. Where would I put the information on Italy? It could belong in either column. When I start talking about Western Europe, my audience might expect to hear about the Italian market only to find I don't discuss it until I get to the Southern Europe section. When there's overlap between the columns, the architecture, and hence the final pitch, gets confusing.

The notion of being distinct also applies to layer approaches. The ideas in your "Background" layer should be distinct from those in your "What's Changed" layer. The easiest way to do this is to separate those two layers by one of three things:

An event. Events serve as a good break point for placing information in the "Background" or "What's Changed" layer. Everything before the event is background and the event itself and anything happening thereafter is what's changed. The event must be relevant to the story you're telling.

A time period. Time periods are clean breaks. For example, everything that happened last year can be included in the "Background" layer and everything in our forecast for next year could be detailed in "What's Changed."

New information. Learning something new can lead you to make a recommendation. An example of this would be our prior understanding of why consumers buy our product. We used to think they bought based on taste. What's changed is we ran a market research study and learned taste does not drive their purchase. They're buying based upon price. That new information serves to differentiate between background—everything we knew before the market research study—and what's changed, which is the result of the market research study.

If you find your ideas aren't distinct from one another and concepts bleed over from one column or layer into the other, redefine those layers or columns so the concepts are distinct. Reorganize the information in a different arrangement to separate the thoughts. If you're following the earlier guidance of building from the top down and letting the core idea drive your column selection, you should have a good start on your thoughts being distinct in a column approach. If you're precise in describing the event that's occurred or the new information that has come to light that is leading you to recommend your core idea, the layers in your layer approach should be distinct.

Stress Test Your Architecture:
Be *Complete*

Completeness means having *all* the information needed to prove your case. This requires you to fill logic and information gaps in your argument. Every part of your core idea must be supported for your recommendation to withstand the scrutiny it will be subjected to. If you're missing a major supporting element, someone will point out that omission at the most inopportune moment. Typically their question comes up during your final presentation. When you can't address their question, your entire argument collapses and your request for approval is denied.

The first pass at completeness is easy. Look at your core idea and ensure every concept you cover in it has support somewhere in the architecture below. If your core idea is "We should launch a new website because we'll increase sales by X% and add Y new customers per month" you'll need support for three concepts somewhere in your architecture: the new website launch, the sales increase, and adding new customers. If any of those concepts aren't supported in your architecture, then your thinking isn't complete. This notion of completeness applies to every level of your architecture too. If you're arguing that building a new website is necessary because your current one is outdated, you'll need support within that section proving you have the capability and budget to build the new site. You also need to support your assessment that the current website is outdated. When you build your architecture from the top down, most of this completeness requirement will take care of itself.

The second pass of completeness is more difficult. You're looking to fill major information gaps that must be addressed for your core idea to hold true. This is hard to do because by definition you're not aware of what you're missing. If you knew something was missing, you would fill in that information gap! There are two ways to identify and fill these information gaps.

First, step back from your architecture and assess it critically. Pretend you're one of your stakeholders and ask yourself what they would expect you to include in your recommendation. Legal might ask you to look at whether or not your idea adheres to industry regulations. Human resources might ask you to determine your idea's people impacts, and IT would want you to analyze your recommendation's technology budget impacts. By looking at your architecture with this critical eye, you'll be able to fill several gaps in your thinking to make your architecture more complete.

Second, when you go through the process of syndicating your idea in future steps, your colleagues will identify gaps in your thinking and suggest how you can fill them in. Their lens on the world is different than yours. They'll see points you're missing in your architecture and can suggest ways for you to fill those information gaps. You'll get their perspectives later in the structured thought process, and when you do, you'll come back to your architecture and update it.

Whew! Building an architecture is a lot of work. It's hard to do and requires you to think critically about how you'll make your case. The good news is once you've created your architecture, the rest of the structured thought process is relatively easy. Your architecture will guide the creation of your story, your analytical efforts, and dictate your final presentation's flow. Your investment of time in getting your architecture right will pay large dividends in terms of efficiency and effectiveness as you advance your pitch through the approval process. A solid architecture focuses your analysis, prevents rework, and gets your audience to yes on your first attempt at pitching your idea.

7

Layer and *Column* Architectures

The *Layer* Architecture

Layer architectures are great for educating an audience that's unfamiliar with your subject. They're also effective for persuading an audience that will be resistant to your idea. A layer architecture works in these situations because you're meeting the audience where they are and guiding them to where you want them to be. That destination is your core idea. For an audience that's not grounded in your subject matter, the "Background" layer will give them context and point them toward your core idea. For an audience that's resistant, the "What's Changed" layer should drive them to action.

The Ungrounded Audience

The "Background" layer connects your idea to an audience that's unfamiliar with it. That layer creates a common understanding of the issue. Without the "Background," your audience will never understand your recommendation and therefore won't be able to approve it. Imagine a scenario where we're making a recommendation to hire five new people for our department. We want to do this because the amount of work our team is being asked to perform has increased in the last year and is forecast to increase further in the future. In this case, our stakeholder—who happens to be our manager's new boss—isn't opposed to the idea but they aren't familiar enough with the situation to make a decision. They recently took over their position after transferring from another department. We could use an architecture like the one on the next page to make our pitch.

●◆

In our "Background" layer we ground our stakeholder on how our team works and how our work impacts company performance. We explain how our current staffing has met the company's needs in the past and up to the present day. With this grounding, our stakeholder can now understand the rest of our recommendation and approve our request for additional personnel. If our stakeholder didn't understand our team's role and how it's connected to company performance, our pitch might come across as us complaining about how hard our jobs are. The layer architecture builds a bridge of understanding from our stakeholder's uninformed state to a position where they have an appropriate amount of context surrounding our recommendation.

Core Idea
We should hire five new team members because we'll be able to meet increased processing demands and help the company achieve its sales and profit goals.

What's Changed?
- Document processing volumes are continuing to increase and we're forecasting a personnel shortage for next year.
- If we have a personnel shortage, we won't be able to achieve our service level goals, and company performance will suffer in the form of lower sales and profits.

Background
- Our team has twenty-seven personnel who conduct document processing activities. We've been at that staffing level for the last four years.
- Document processing volumes have been steadily increasing over that time period, but we've been able to meet that demand and achieve our service level requirements.
- Our team's performance is measured by service level agreements, and we consistently meet our goals. When we meet our goals, the company does well. If we fail to meet goals, company sales and profit performance suffer.

Figure 7.1

If you're making a recommendation to an uninformed audience, look at the "Background" layer from their perspective. Write down the critical pieces of information they need to understand the situation. You may feel the ideas you write down seem too basic to be worth sharing. That's because your perspective is clouding the situation. You already know all these facts and have known them for a long time. These are the basics of your job. Including this information might feel like a waste of your stakeholder's time. But when you look at it from your stakeholder's perspective, this new information should pique their interest. Write this section as if you're educating a new team member about the work your organization does or the situation you're facing. This "Background" layer has to take your audience from a position of knowing nothing to one where they understand enough context for your recommendation to make sense.

The Resistant Audience

There will be many situations where you're pitching your idea to an audience that's opposed to approving it. There can be many reasons behind their reluctance to approve your recommendation. They may oppose your idea because you're competing for the same resources; it causes uncomfortable change for them; they believe you're taking on excessive risk; or they simply don't like you. Yes, I've seen audiences oppose an idea based upon interpersonal squabbles! Whatever their reason for resistance, your task is to overcome it and get your pitch approved. The "What's Changed" layer is a major step toward overcoming their objections.

For the resistant audience, the "Background" layer serves to build a common understanding. Make sure what you share in that layer is not at all controversial. You're trying to get your stakeholder's head nodding up and down in agreement from the beginning of your pitch. If you put controversial information in your "Background" layer, you risk alienating them right from the start. Unlike your ungrounded audience, your resistant audience might be familiar with the information you share in your "Background" layer, and that's okay. You're trying to demonstrate you share a similar view of the situation. Beware of sharing information that's *too* basic; you might insult an audience that's already predisposed to disagreeing with you. Once you're convinced your resistant audience agrees with your background, it's time to move them toward your core idea. Your "What's Changed" layer is the device for starting that movement. A good "What's Changed" layer makes it clear that action must be taken.

Effective points to include in your "What's Changed" layer are events and new information. Events like market changes, new regulations, business performance shortfalls, and competitive actions can all serve to prod your resistant audience forward. New information like consumer research findings, scientific discoveries, test results, and competitive intelligence can encourage a resistant audience to act. An effective "What's Changed" layer makes your audience understand inaction is not a viable choice.

Using your "What's Changed" layer to prompt action has a connection to the well-known metaphor of the burning platform. In that metaphor, your audience is trapped atop a tall, wooden platform in the middle of the ocean. To make matters worse, there's a school of hungry sharks swimming around the platform. In your audience's mind, those sharks represent your idea. To them, your idea is unpleasant at best and terrifying at worst. Your audience is quite content sitting on that platform away from the danger of the sharks. The platform is their comfort zone while the water is their danger zone. Your task is to move your audience to action. You want them to get over their fear of the sharks and get in the water. You have to push them out of their comfort zone and get them to face the risks of their danger zone. In the burning platform metaphor, your audience is likely to take their chances and jump in the water then swim for safety if the platform happens to catch fire. A good "What's Changed" layer is the match that sets the platform aflame. You need to show the audience it's more dangerous to sit on the burning platform doing nothing than it is to take their chances in the dangerous waters. On the next page is an example architecture that achieves this desired effect.

●◆

If your reluctant stakeholder is the packaging manager who oversees labeling processes, they'd prefer to keep the labels the way they are. Making changes to labels is costly and time consuming. You can acknowledge this fact in your "Background" layer. The packaging manager will violently agree with it. Such changes will lead to extra work, longer hours, missed budgets, and frustrated employees. No manager in their right mind would change their labels if those were the consequences! Even if the packaging manager saw a competitor get hit with fines and face business interruption, he would still be reluctant to change his labels without being forced to do so. Your job is to pitch the recommendation in a way that demonstrates failing to act *now* has worse consequences than making the changes *before* you're forced to make them.

Core Idea

We should change our labels immediately to avoid $XMM in issue resolution costs and $YMM in losses stemming from removing our products from store shelves.

What's Changed?

- The Food and Drug Administration (FDA) recently ruled our biggest competitor's labels were noncompliant and ordered their products removed from stores until the labels were changed.
- The FDA hasn't indicated they're looking at our products, but if they do and they make a similar ruling it will cost us $XMM to rectify the issue and lead to $YMM in losses from pulling our products off store shelves.

Background

- Our product labels contain both marketing information and nutrition information.
- The FDA oversees what we can and cannot claim on our packaging with respect to nutrition and ingredient performance. We believe our labels are compliant with their rules.
- The nutrition information and ingredient claims on our product labels are virtually identical to those of our biggest competitor.
- Making changes to our labels is costly, time consuming, and creates the risk of customers not purchasing our products.

Figure 7.2

In your "What's Changed" layer, spell out the negative consequences of inaction. By waiting for the FDA to force your hand, the organization would face staggering losses. Not only would there be large issue-resolution costs stemming from a frantic project and fines, but you'd also face millions in losses. You would have to recall noncompliant product from stores and destroy it, then replace it with new product bearing compliant labels. During the time your product is unavailable in stores, you face the risk of competitors stealing market share.

The flames on the platform are getting hot for the packaging manager! While there's no guarantee the FDA will rule you have to modify your labels, the risk of them forcing you to change is scary enough to drive the packaging manager to act. He would rather make the change now than be known as the guy who opposed the change when he had a chance to make it without suffering massive losses. Your "What's Changed" layer drives action because it changes the packaging manager's perspective on the issue. He now sees inaction as more dangerous than taking preemptive action despite the turmoil acting now will create. Once the balance shifts from inaction to action, the packaging manager is open to supporting your core idea.

The layer approach is an ideal choice for moving an audience from where they are to where you want them to be. Whether they're unfamiliar with the recommendation or resistant to it, this approach enables you to put yourself in their position and travel alongside them on their path to approving your pitch. Your ungrounded audience will find the "Background" layer more informative. The resistant audience will be more compelled by your "What's Changed" layer. The layer approach is an effective technique for getting both of those audience types to agree with your core idea.

The *Column* Architecture

Column architectures are well suited for communicating with audiences that already have the context related to your pitch. You should use a column approach with stakeholders who want to get to the answer quickly. Many times your boss is a good target for this approach. They understand the situation and have little patience for being provided information they already know. They'd prefer you go straight to your recommendation and then share the facts supporting it. But be careful! Don't always assume they have context. Even though you've pitched them with a column approach for the last nine recommendations you've brought them, they might be unfamiliar with the subject matter of the tenth pitch. Assess each pitch situation individually. While your audience may be predisposed to want a column approach, the better you're able to discern their support level and knowledge level, the better you'll be able to select the most effective architecture for your pitch.

The easiest way to create your column approach is to start with your core idea. One technique for creating this architecture is to underline the major concepts in the core idea and create a separate column for each concept. A second approach is to look for themes in your core idea and create columns related to each theme. Since I've already shared a column approach example using this first technique, let's explore the second technique of creating columns based upon themes. Let's build a column architecture to support the following core idea:

We should market and sell our Doodliebop to teens, young adults, and grandparents because it will drive $XMM in sales, $YMM in profits, and expand margins by Z%.

We could group supports into three columns. One column is the product sales and marketing activities we'll perform. That theme is based upon the point "We should market and sell our Doodliebop." A second column will cover the segments we're marketing to. The information about "teens, young adults, and grandparents" points to this market segment theme. A third column will explain the financial benefits of taking this action. That theme came from the points about "$XMM in sales, $YMM in profits, and expand margins by Z%." The architecture could look like Figure 7.3 on the next page.

●◆

All three columns are distinct from one another. One is about the item we're selling, another about who we're selling it to, and the third is about the money we'll make from selling it. Those are separate concepts. This architecture is also complete. Every point in the core idea is supported somewhere in the columns below it.

As far as the bullet points contained in each column, some come from the core idea. Others are hypotheses as to information we could include that would support the column containing the point. For now, these are information placeholders. We'll prove or disprove these points in future steps. What's important at this stage is the construction of a basic argument for how we'll prove our core idea. Once we have the initial argument fleshed out in the architecture, we're ready to move to the next step.

Core Idea
We should market and sell our Doodliebop to teens, young adults, and grandparents because it will drive $XMM in sales, $YMM in profits, and expand margins by Z%.

Product	Segments	Financials
• Our newest product launch is called the Doodliebop. • We should conduct mass-media marketing activities to support the launch. • We should engage in selling activities to get retailers to carry Doodliebops in stores.	• Our primary target segment should be teens. • Our secondary segment should be young adults. • Our tertiary segment should be grandparents who buy it for their grandchildren.	• The Doodliebop should generate $XMM in sales. • Those sales should generate $YMM in profits. • Given this is a high-margin product, these sales should expand our margins by Z%.

Figure 7.3

Considerations for Building a Good Column Architecture

Although a column architecture is simple to construct, there are a few fine points to consider when building one. If you keep the following thoughts in mind while building your column architecture, you'll find it's easier to understand and remember, and more compelling to your audience.

Column sequence. When constructing a column architecture, don't worry about the sequence of the columns. There's no need to think through the order in which you'll share them yet. You'll make that decision later in the process once you have a better sense for your audience and what points you want to emphasize. That said, if there is an obvious sequence to communicating your columns, by all means, construct your architecture accordingly. In Figure 7.3, it makes sense to share information about the Doodliebop product before discussing the market segments. It's also logical to have the resultant financial results come last; therefore the left-to-right column sequence makes sense. If you're not sure how to sequence your columns yet, leave that decision for later in the process.

Number of columns. Think about the last few times you went grocery shopping. If you only needed two or three items, it was easy to remember them without writing them down. If you needed six or more items, you likely created a list to ensure you didn't go home without one of the items you needed. This list dynamic happens because it's hard to retain more than five items in short-term memory. Let's conduct a small experiment related to this point.

Below is a list of fifteen items. Set a timer for one minute. Once you start the timer, review the list and do your best to memorize all fifteen items. Don't write anything down, only read the list and memorize. After one minute, close the book and, in two minutes, write down as many items as you can remember from the list. Ready? Go!

Laughing	Mules	Diamonds
Fish	Daisies	Dogs
Dancing	Horses	Sleeping
Turtles	Shopping	Roses
Scarves	Chocolates	Writing

Okay. Let's do the same exercise with a different set of ideas. Again, you have one minute to memorize the following words, then close the book and write down as many items as you can remember in two minutes. Go!

Fruits	Names	Places
Raspberry	Kendall	Park
Coconut	Elroy	Office
Blueberry	Danielle	City
Pineapple	Michael	Airport
Peach	Alexandra	Beach

In the first exercise, how many items did you remember? Five? Seven? If you're like most people I give this exercise to, you remembered seven to nine items. Think about the experience of trying to memorize those concepts. Did you find yourself trying to memorize every item individually? Did you try to create logical groups for the concepts or did you try to burn each word into your memory one at a time? How did you feel when you did the exercise? Was it confusing or frustrating? If you didn't get all fifteen, did you feel disappointed?

Now recall your experience with the second exercise. How many items did you remember? Did you notice this time you had eighteen items to remember in the second exercise versus the fifteen in the first? I added three column headings that you needed to remember in addition to the items on the list. Did you remember more items in the second exercise than you did in the first? When you spent the two minutes writing down your list, did you write a category, write in all the items in that category, then repeat the same process for the other two categories? Was it easier and less frustrating when you realized you had to remember items in three groups versus fifteen individual items?

Imagine if the first exercise were presented to you this way:

Actions	Animals	Gifts
Laughing	Turtles	Diamonds
Sleeping	Dogs	Daisies
Dancing	Horses	Chocolates
Shopping	Fish	Roses
Writing	Mules	Scarves

It would have been easier to remember those items if they were categorized, right? Conduct this experiment with your team. See if they get the same results and have the same reactions you did. I'm willing to bet they do because most people tend to process information the same way.

Numerous psychological studies have concluded the human brain has the capacity to remember a limit of four to seven concepts from a given idea set. After seven concepts, people start forgetting things. You should be mindful of this dynamic when deciding how many columns to include in your architecture. I encourage you to choose between two and five columns. You want your audience to remember your recommendation. If you throw eight different columns at them, they'll retain some of the information but then reach a point where they're overwhelmed by how much you're presenting to them. They'll feel the same way you probably felt with the list of fifteen items in the first exercise. By limiting the number of columns well below the threshold of memory, your audience will be able to absorb the information more easily. They'll find it easier to remember your ideas too. They might not remember all the sub-bullets in a column but they'll remember more of your recommendation if it's arranged into fewer groupings.

Completeness of columns. Once you've constructed your column architecture, be rigorous about assessing it for completeness. That means going back to your core idea and making sure *everything* in your core idea is included in the architecture below it. The most common mistake people make is forgetting to include a column to support the hypothesis part of the core idea. Here's what happens. They have a core idea that states:

We should change our emergency room screening process because it will increase revenues by $XMM, improve patient satisfaction by Y%, and raise staff morale by Z%.

The first reaction people have is to create columns below this core idea related to revenues, patient satisfaction, and staff morale. That's correct. What often gets forgotten, though, is the need for a column to support the changes to the ER screening process. Remember to include support for your *entire* core idea.

You might decide not to give a core idea concept its own entire column but instead choose to support it somewhere in another column. In this example, you could include support for the ER screening-process changes within the column for patient satisfaction. One of your points in that column could be a description of the current screening process and how it frustrates patients. A second point could be the screening process changes you plan on making. That approach would satisfy the need to be complete without creating a separate column to support the screening process element in the core idea. The bottom line is make sure you support all your core idea's components somewhere in your column architecture.

The column approach is a great way to give your audience the information they need in a clear and concise manner. When you use it, you avoid boring them with information they already know. The information you do share is direct, and this architecture demonstrates you respect their existing knowledge base. A column architecture leads to short conversations and quick approval for your pitch.

Create a *Story*

Congratulations! You've completed the most challenging step of the structured thought process. Building your architecture will take time and effort. If you've invested in it properly, your architecture will make the rest of the process easy. Once you've built your architecture, the next step is to create your story. Your story will be derived from your architecture. You spent time building a logical architecture designed to meet your audience's information needs. This is where that time investment pays off.

Your story is a longhand draft of your recommendation. It should be a simple narrative designed to get your audience from wherever they are to a place where they understand and approve your recommendation. When you write your story, I encourage you to write it in your preferred word-processing program, the most common of which are Microsoft Word and Google Docs. Some people prefer writing their story in an email. I prefer Word or Google Docs because it's easier to edit my story as I refine it in future steps.

Your story will look more like an outline than it will resemble a block of prose like you're reading in this book. The story will have major points supported by subpoints supported by other subpoints. I'll share several example stories in this chapter to give you a feel for what a good story looks like.

When you write your story, use complete sentences. Your goal is to leave nothing open to interpretation because many times that's where misunderstandings begin. A complete sentence reduces uncertainty about what you're saying. A bullet point can mean different things to different people because it leaves out important context for interpreting the information. In your first draft of your story, focus on creating a narrative that flows. I emphasize the word "draft" as I describe the story. Your story *will* change as you move through the process. You'll have conversations, conduct analyses, and learn new information that will lead to changes in your story. Some changes will be small while others might completely alter the story you're going to tell. What's important at this stage is getting a draft narrative written down so you have a clear understanding of your pitch's flow.

Don't worry about word choice. You shouldn't be wordsmithing at this stage. If you're struggling with whether to write "significantly" or "dramatically" in one of your points, write "a lot" and move on. Why? Because you might conduct one analysis in future steps and find out a graph goes down when you expected it to go up. That analysis then nullifies your "significantly" or your "dramatically." Wordsmithing at this stage often ends up being wasted effort. You'll have plenty of time to choose the perfect words when you craft your final communication. For now, focus on getting the story's logical flow correct.

Go From *Layer* Architecture to Story

If you chose to use a layer architecture, it's a simple manipulation to go from architecture to story. You'll take your architecture, invert it, and then write. The "Background" section will come first, then the "What's Changed" section, and finally your core idea. A story based upon a layer architecture will read like the stories you heard in your childhood:

"Once upon a time ("Background")..."
"And then something happened ("What's Changed")..."
"So our heroes saved the day by doing (Core Idea)..."

This is why it may have felt more comfortable reading a layer architecture from bottom to top in prior steps. It's a logical flow to start with your "Background," explain the conflict of "What's Changed," and then resolve the issue with your core idea.

Let's look at how a layer architecture we created earlier can be transformed into a story. Remember the pitch we made in Figure 7.1 (p. 113) for hiring more people to deal with increased document processing volumes? Here's the story based on that layer architecture:

> **Our historical staffing levels have enabled us to meet processing demand and achieve our goals.**
>
> - Our team has twenty-seven personnel who conduct document processing activities. We've been at that staffing level for the last four years.
> - Document processing volumes have been increasing over that time period, but we've been able to meet demand and achieve our service level requirements.
> - Our team's performance is measured by service level agreements, and we consistently meet our goals.
> - When we meet our goals, the company does well. If we fail to meet goals, company sales and profit performance suffer.
>
> **Processing-volume increases are threatening the company's ability to meet its financial goals.**
>
> - Document processing volumes are continuing to increase and we're forecasting a personnel shortage for next year.
> - If we have a personnel shortage, we won't be able to achieve our service level goals, and company performance will suffer in the form of lower sales and profits.
>
> **We should hire five new team members because we'll be able to meet increased processing demands and help the company achieve its sales and profit goals.**

I replaced the words "Background" and "What's Changed" with a sentence summarizing that particular portion of the architecture. The summary I provided is an interpretation of the supporting points contained in that section. This interpretation is a necessary step as you transform your architecture into a story. One desired outcome for your story is your audience draws the conclusion you want them to draw. To achieve that goal, interpret the information in each layer and tell your audience how to think about the details you're about to share with them. If you don't interpret the information for them, they'll interpret it for themselves. I often joke that independent thought is a dangerous thing and you should squash it at every turn because when people think, bad things can happen. While that's a provocative and cheeky statement, there's an element of truth to it as it relates to telling your story.

If you only write "Background" or "What's changed?" then present a series of bullet points from your architecture, there's a risk your audience could interpret those bullet points differently than you want them to. This is analogous to the grouping exercise we did related to golf and American football versus poker and animals. Without the right lens, the audience interprets those groups based on their own experience, which may be different than the groups you want them to look at. The same principle applies to transforming your architecture into a story. Write a synthesis of the supporting points for each section in a way that directs your audience toward your ultimate recommendation.

You'll need to strike a balance between synthesis and wordsmithing. While you need to summarize the points in a particular layer to guide your audience to your conclusion, don't invest excessive effort in perfecting the summary. When you feel like you've got enough of an interpretation to guide your audience, move on to the next step. You'll have a chance to wordsmith and perfect the summary later in the process.

In addition to sequencing the major elements of your story in the "Background," "What's Changed," then core idea sequence, put your supporting points in an order that makes sense too. In the item processing story, note the point about the team meeting its goals comes before the point about the company's goals. That's a logical progression. If that sequence were reversed, the story wouldn't flow as well. Be deliberate about the order in which you discuss your supporting points. That sequence can either improve or disrupt your story's flow.

By way of another example, on the next page is the story from Figure 7.2 (p. 117) about changing our labels to avoid losses and FDA fines.

•❖

See how the synthesis of each section guides the audience toward the core idea? If you refer back to the original architecture, you'll see I reordered the points in the "Background" section to make them flow more naturally. The resequencing is a small refinement but it moves the story closer to becoming an elegant pitch. When you finish writing a story based on a layer approach, step away from it for a few hours, then come back and read it from the top all the way through to the core idea. Don't stop reading until you get to the end. Does the story flow from one point to the next? Does everything feel like it's in the proper sequence? Does your core idea seem to be the only logical conclusion to arrive at based upon the "Background" and "What's Changed" sections? If the

Our labels are similar to our competitor's and are compliant with FDA requirements.

- Our product labels contain both marketing information and nutrition information.

- The FDA oversees what we can and cannot claim on our packaging with respect to nutrition and ingredient performance. We believe our labels are compliant with their rules.

- Making changes to our labels is costly, time consuming, and creates the risk of customers not purchasing our products.

- The nutrition information and ingredient claims on our product labels are virtually identical to our biggest competitor's.

But the FDA's recent ruling about our competitor's labels creates a large financial risk for us.

- The FDA recently ruled our biggest competitor's labels were noncompliant and ordered their products be removed from stores until the labels were changed.

- The FDA hasn't indicated they're looking at our products, but if they do and they make a similar ruling, it will cost us $XMM to rectify the issue and lead to $YMM in losses from pulling our products off store shelves.

We should change our labels immediately to avoid $XMM in issue resolution costs and $YMM in losses stemming from removing our products from store shelves.

answer to any of these questions is no, continue refining the story until the flow feels right. Getting the flow right will go a long way toward crafting a clear and compelling final communication.

Some people argue the core idea should come first no matter what and that you should never invert your layer architecture. I fundamentally disagree. Imagine a situation where your audience is highly resistant to your core idea. If the first thing they read is a statement they disagree with, they'll likely shut down and get argumentative. That defeats the purpose of crafting your story in a manner designed to make them receptive to your controversial idea. If your audience lacks context and you again lead with your core idea rather than invert the architecture and start with the "Background," you could confuse them right from the start, which will make influencing them that much more difficult. Hopefully, this logic makes the rationale for inverting a layer architecture obvious.

Go From *Column* Architecture to Story

When going from column architecture to story, there's no inversion of the architecture. With a column approach, you'll first write your core idea and follow it with your columns. Remember, you're using a column approach because your audience is already grounded and they want to get to the answer quickly. You can't get there any faster than giving them your recommendation as the first sentence!

For example, using the column architecture from Figure 7.3 (p. 121), here's the story explaining how we should sell and market Doodliebops:

We should market and sell our Doodliebop to teens, young adults, and grandparents because it will drive $XMM in sales, $YMM in profits, and expand margins by Z%.

A successful Doodliebop new product launch requires mass-media marketing and targeted selling to retailers.

- Our newest product launch is called the Doodliebop.
- We should conduct mass-media marketing activities to support the launch.
- We should engage in selling activities to get retailers to carry Doodliebops in stores.

Our sales and marketing efforts need to focus on three lucrative market segments.

- Our primary target segment should be teens.
- Our secondary segment should be young adults.
- Our tertiary segment should be grandparents who buy the toy for their grandchildren.

The Doodliebop product launch should yield attractive financial results.

- The Doodliebop should generate $XMM in sales.
- Those sales should generate $YMM in profits.
- Given this is a high-margin product, these sales should expand our margins by Z%.

The story based on this column architecture gets to the point quickly. The audience knows the recommendation in the first sentence and the points below it support the case. The column headings we had in the architecture are now complete thoughts. Instead of only listing "Product," "Segments," and "Financials," they're now complete sentences that guide the audience to the conclusion we want them to draw.

One important decision you'll need to make when transforming a column architecture into a story is the sequence in which you'll arrange your columns. Earlier I mentioned you would determine column sequence later in the process. This is the time to do that. Your default approach may be to list the columns in your story in the same sequence they appear in from left to right on your architecture because that's the natural direction in which we read. Don't succumb to the default mindset. Instead, consider your audience and sequence your columns accordingly.

In the above Doodliebop example, the story sequence makes sense if you're pitching your idea to the Doodliebop product manager. Why? Because the points you're covering first are all about launching the new product. That's the most important point—to the product manager—therefore it should be the first point you talk about. If the audience is your chief financial officer, that story won't be as effective. As written, you'll talk about product launch and sales and marketing activities before you touch on the new product's financial characteristics. Your CFO might become irritated because you're not addressing the most important aspect of the launch—the expected financial results—first. If you know you're pitching to the CFO, your story should look like this:

We should market and sell our Doodliebop to teens, young adults, and grandparents because it will drive $XMM in sales, $YMM in profits, and expand margins by Z%.

The Doodliebop product launch should yield attractive financial results.

- The Doodliebop should generate $XMM in sales.
- Those sales should generate $YMM in profits.
- Given this is a high-margin product, these sales should expand our margins by Z%.

A successful Doodliebop new product launch requires mass-media marketing and targeted selling to retailers.

- Our newest product launch is called the Doodliebop.
- We should conduct mass-media marketing activities to support the launch.
- We should engage in selling activities to get retailers to carry Doodliebops in stores.

Our sales and marketing efforts need to focus on three lucrative market segments.

- Our primary target segment should be teens.
- Our secondary segment should be young adults.
- Our tertiary segment should be grandparents who buy the toy for their grandchildren.

By putting the financials first, you're addressing your audience's most pressing need before getting into topics they might be less interested in. Yes, this means you'll need to construct separate stories for separate audiences the same way you created separate architectures for separate audiences. The better your story meets your audience's information needs and reflects their interests or biases, the more likely it is they'll approve your pitch.

Sometimes your columns will need to follow a natural sequence in the story. If you can't understand column #2 without first understanding column #3, then put column #3 first, followed by column #2, because that order is logical. For example, look at our architecture from Figure 6.4 (p. 98) where we're pitching the purchase of a new dialer. Our story could look like the one on the next page.

◗

We should buy a new dialer from Vendor ABC to reduce our losses by $XMM per year.

If we buy a new dialer, we should get it from Vendor ABC.

- Vendor ABC sells high-quality dialers.
- Vendor ABC has competitive pricing.
- Only one other vendor's products are approved by our IT group, Vendor DEF.
- Vendor DEF's product is inferior to vendor ABC's.

There are three good reasons for us to buy a new dialer.

- Our dialer is old and keeps breaking down.
- There are newer and better dialers on the market.
- A better, more reliable dialer will improve our collections performance.

A new dialer will reduce our losses.

- Our losses have increased by $ZMM this year.
- A new dialer could deliver loss reduction of $XMM per year.

As written, that story doesn't flow well. After our core idea, the story covers which vendor to buy a dialer from and then makes the argument for why we need a new dialer. That story is not as logical as it would be if we flipped the sequence to the next story (turn the page).

We should buy a new dialer from Vendor ABC to reduce our losses by $XMM per year.

There are three good reasons for us to buy a new dialer.

- Our dialer is old and keeps breaking down.
- There are newer and better dialers on the market.
- A better, more reliable dialer will improve our collections performance.

If we buy a new dialer, we should get it from Vendor ABC.

- Vendor ABC sells high-quality dialers.
- Vendor ABC has competitive pricing.
- Only one other vendor's products are approved by our IT group, Vendor DEF.
- Vendor DEF's product is inferior to vendor ABC's.

A new dialer will reduce our losses.

- Our losses have increased by $ZMM this year.
- A new dialer could deliver loss reduction of $XMM per year.

That story has a better flow than the first one. First the case is made for a new dialer and then the recommendation of which vendor to purchase from is made. This is a more logical sequence.

Once you've completed your first draft of your story based on a column architecture, pretend you're your target audience. Read the story from their perspective. Ask yourself if the story has a logical flow. Does the story address your audience's most pressing concerns first or when logically appropriate? Does the core idea make sense right from the start? Do the points supporting the core idea back up the recommendation? Keep refining your story until you can answer all these questions in the affirmative.

Crafting *Stories* for Emails, Voicemails, and Business Cases

The notion of creating a story based upon an architecture isn't limited to building a presentation. You can use architecture to create stories for other common communication vehicles like emails, voicemails, and business cases. The simplest way to illustrate this is to look at a poor example then rework it into a compelling pitch. Imagine you received the following email:

> Hi Heather.
>
> I got the cost estimates for the project. Judy finished the analysis yesterday. She got it done a day early. I think this is a good idea. The financials show a $4MM profit increase over a three-year period assuming a 12% market share increase. Market share now is growing at 5%. Prithviraj had thoughts on this too. We need to talk to him; he thinks 12% is achievable. By the way, the new brand materials will be available next week to support this launch. The color scheme is really cool. It's bright orange on seafoam! Take a look at the attached materials. I'll talk to you soon.
>
> Dave

While Dave has shared a lot of great information, it's not clear what he's asking for. The variety of facts gets confusing, and it's not easy to see how every fact is relevant. While the bright-orange-on-seafoam color scheme sounds pleasant and Dave is excited about the colors, the scheme's inclusion is distracting.

If Dave had spent time creating an architecture and drafting his email based upon the story the architecture guided him toward, the email could have looked like this:

Hi Heather.

I'd like your approval for the new service line launch because it's projected to have a $4MM profit impact (supporting materials attached). Please reply with "approve" to this email by COB tomorrow, and we'll get the service line launched by the target date. Here are a few points from the attached presentation to inform this decision:

- The financials show a $4MM profit increase over a three-year period.

- The launch assumes a 12% market share increase, which Prithviraj believes is reasonable.

- The new brand materials will be available next week to support this launch.

Please let me know your decision by 5 PM tomorrow. Thanks.

Dave

In this example, the recommendation is the first sentence Heather will read. The first bullet point pushes her button for increased profits. Supporting points about profits, market share, and brand support for the launch follow. You can likely draw the column architecture this email was based upon. Dave then closes the email with a clear deadline for action. This second email eliminates distractions like the bright orange and seafoam color scheme. It's a cleaner pitch than the first email. The chances of Dave getting his idea approved are higher for the second email than the first. The time he took to create an architecture and turn it into a story that he sent via email is the reason Heather is more likely to approve the idea.

Architecture and stories can make your voicemails more effective too. When I was a consultant, we had a guy on our team who tended to leave long, rambling voicemails. I'll refer to him as Jeff. Kevin, the senior partner on our project, wasn't fond of receiving Jeff's messages. The first time he got one, he replied to Jeff and said, "Thanks for the update. Next time you update me, can you be a little more concise and to the point? Thanks."

Jeff's next update was a little better but still tended to ramble on. Kevin again replied with a request for a more succinct message. The third voicemail Jeff left for Kevin was another unstructured update. Kevin had had enough. He replied to Jeff and said, "I've asked you several times to ramble less and put more structure to your messages. Obviously, I'm not making myself clear on this. What I'd like you to do is transcribe the last voicemail you sent me—including all the "ums" and "uhs"—then rewrite it in a structured email I can understand and reply to." Was the response harsh? Yes. Did Jeff deserve this punishment? Absolutely.

Even though Jeff knew how to create an architecture and tell a story, he only applied those skills to his presentations. He failed to translate those techniques to his other communications, which frustrated his audience. The reason Jeff had numerous "ums" and "uhs" in his voicemails was because he didn't know what he was going to say next. Those verbal pauses occurred because he was collecting his thoughts and thinking about the next point he needed to make. From that day on, Jeff would write out his story before leaving an update voicemail for the partners on our project. While scripting his message cost him additional time to compose his thoughts, his efforts paid off. His voicemails got shorter and easier to understand. After practicing these habits over time, he found he received faster replies to his messages and positive feedback about the clarity of his communications.

Like emails and voicemails, business cases can benefit from having an architecture and a story. For example, read the following business case:

This idea has many benefits:
- Customers will spend less time activating their service, which will cost us less money.
- Our service technicians will deal with happier customers and their morale will increase.
- Service technicians' time spent on installations will decrease by 5%.
- Customers will be happier and retention will increase by 12%.
- Service call costs will decrease by $5MM.
- Brand image will be enhanced.
- Service technicians will solve more difficult problems, which will increase job satisfaction.
- Better retention will increase profits by $5MM.

There seem to be many benefits to pursuing the idea, but all those bullet points and numbers can be overwhelming. The business case lacks architecture and a clear story. Contrast that business case with this one:

We should pursue this initiative for three reasons:

- **Economic benefits: $10MM profit increase/year**
  - Better retention will increase profits by $5MM.
  - Service call costs will decrease by $5MM.
  - Service technicians' time spent on installations will decrease by 5%.
- **Customer benefits: enhanced relationships**
  - Happier customers will result in a 12% retention increase.
  - Brand image will be enhanced.
- **Service technician benefits: improved morale**
  - Our service technicians will deal with happier customers, and their morale will increase.
  - Service technicians will solve more difficult problems, which will increase their job satisfaction.

There are three compelling reasons for pursuing this case: it's worth $10MM; our customers will be happier; and our service technicians will have higher morale. While you may not remember all the supporting bullet points below those three major points, you'll likely recall the primary reasons the recommendation is being made. Architecture makes this business case more compelling.

Now, go back and look at the first business case and compare it to the second. Do you notice anything? All the information is the same! The first business case is an unstructured list of facts. The second business case puts structure to those facts in the form of an architecture that's then transformed into a simple story. Which business case took longer to write—the first or the second? Why, the second of course! It required thought. But that investment of thought is likely to yield quick approval for the business case. Pitching the first business case will be more difficult because it's unstructured. Architecture and a clear story matter regardless of the communication vehicle you're using for making your pitch.

Guiding *Principles* for Writing Your Story

Crafting clear and compelling stories is something you can improve upon over time. The more architectures you convert to stories and the more presentations, emails, voicemails, and business cases you practice on, the faster you'll build your skills. A few guiding principles can help you achieve proficiency more rapidly.

Don't change the architecture! If your architecture is logical, don't change it. The story flows from it. You invested time and thought into creating an architecture that supports your core idea. You've assessed your audience and what information they need, as well as the sequence in which they need it. Many times I see people make the mistake of building a great architecture that they ignore and write a story that's completely detached from the architecture they created. When you move from architecture to story, get the return on your time and effort investments. Let the architecture drive the story's creation.

Keep the story simple. You're not writing a novel. Write directly and simply. If you do, your story will be easier for your audience to follow. Use short sentences. Focus on your recommendation's most relevant elements and eliminate distractions. The easier your story is to understand, the faster your audience can approve your idea.

Stay out of the details. Stories look like outlines. You'll have your major points supported by subpoints further supported by sub-subpoints. Some people feel the urge to include every last detail in their story. That's not necessary. As you write your story, evaluate each bullet point you include. If your story will become a presentation, there's a technique you can use to determine when you've gone deep enough into your bullet points. When you can "see" the chart or analysis that would support a bullet, stop adding supporting points and move to the next step. Your story defines your pitch's flow. You'll be able to include all the supporting details as pages in the presentation. There's no need to detail all of them in your story's narrative.

Getting your story to flow goes a long way toward making your final pitch elegant. By letting your architecture determine the first draft of your story, you'll build your argument's logic into the final communication. Time spent thinking through how you want to shape your audience's perspective will influence the way they'll interpret the data you share with them. Begin shaping those perspectives when you write the story. And remember, treat *all* your communications as opportunities to tell a story. The famous business leader Lee Iacocca said, "You can have brilliant ideas, but if you can't get them across, your ideas won't get you anywhere." Your story is the vehicle for getting your idea across quickly and clearly.

Refine Your Story

Up to this point in the structured thought process, you've been working alone or within your immediate team. You've not yet sought out external perspectives on your idea. Once you've finished drafting your story, it makes sense—to you. Your story might not make sense to other people. You have context that resides in your mind but not on the written page. When you share your story with someone who is missing this context, the story may not convince them or could confuse them because of these information gaps.

Similarly, you don't have all the context or experience your stakeholders might have. That means they might see gaps in your story that you don't. They may identify contentious points where they disagree with a conclusion you make, or they may not believe a hypothesis you advance. This story refinement step is where you'll identify those gaps, points of disagreement, and new facts to include in your story.

Discussing your story requires you to share your story with people who can broaden and deepen your thinking. You should include individuals who will be stakeholders in the final decision and the decision makers who will approve or disapprove your idea. When you share your story, you're not only enriching your idea. You're building buy-in and support for your recommendation. You're getting people familiar with the recommendation, its rationale, and the facts you plan on using to support your argument. By identifying your audience's concerns before you make your final recommendation, you're able to evaluate and address those issues in your pitch. That should eliminate many of the barriers to pitch approval.

Guiding *Principles* for Your Discussions

These stakeholder conversations will be challenging. Before you begin these discussions, get yourself in the right frame of mind. Your mindset toward these conversations will be a determinant in how successful your efforts are. To work through the challenges you'll face in this step, follow these guiding principles:

It's a preliminary story. During these early conversations, you won't even have data to support your story. That can make your stakeholders uncomfortable. They may not be used to seeing an idea at such an early stage. They might be unfamiliar with a hypothesis-driven approach to making recommendations. You'll need to help them overcome those concerns. To get them past their discomfort related to the absence of data, place caveats around your work's status. When you share your story with them, let them know what stage the idea is at as well as how they can provide productive feedback. For example, you might say something like, "I'd like to share a preliminary idea with you and get your feedback on it. This is an initial hypothesis. I haven't done any analysis yet. I want to get your thoughts on whether I'm answering the right question or not." By saying that, you've managed their expectations related to what information you have or don't have. You've provided specific guidance as to how they can be helpful.

You'll need to get past your own discomfort related to sharing an idea before you've proven it's correct. By letting stakeholders know your work's current status, you can reduce the expectations for completeness or accuracy of your argument. When you tell someone your idea is preliminary and you haven't done any analysis yet, you've lowered their expectations in terms of the rigor you've put into your idea. Remind yourself you're not approaching them for their approval yet. You're trying to get their perspectives and round out your thinking before you expend analytical effort. This should reduce the amount of pressure you feel to be right at this early stage.

Think broadly about who your stakeholders are. Typical syndication processes tend to be vertical. People discuss their idea with their team members, their boss, their boss's boss, and the decision makers above them. Yes, all those individuals provide important input into your story and they're supporters you need to win over to get your pitch approved. I encourage you to think broadly about which stakeholders you involve. Consider other groups who might be impacted by your work in any way and seek out their perspectives. Oftentimes, it's not the direct attack that sinks your pitch. It's the shot from an unexpected direction that blows a hole in your story and causes your entire pitch to collapse. When you look at your recommendation's broader impacts and get support from those who will be affected, you reduce the likelihood of getting your idea shot down because of an unexpected objection.

Your story will change. I've never seen a story remain the same as it goes through this syndication process. Avoid the temptation to resist changing your story based on others' feedback. This is easier said than done. After all the work you've put into your core idea, your architecture, and your story, it's hard to accept suggestions on alternate ways to pitch your idea. That's similar to building the frame for an entire house only to have someone else come along and tell you to rearrange the floor plan because your current layout isn't what the buyer wants. You might feel like all the effort you put into the framing was wasted because now you're doing it all over again. But what if you didn't get that feedback at the framing stage? What if you completed the entire house and had built walls, installed carpet, painted, and furnished it, then the buyer showed up and said, "That's not what I wanted! I wanted the house laid out like this..." That situation makes rearranging your framing seem less painful, doesn't it? Now imagine instead of framing you're rearranging whiteboard drawings and a one-page outline versus rebuilding an entire presentation filled with analyses that took you dozens of hours to complete. There's less wasted effort in the first situation than the second. Be open to changing your story while it's still preliminary.

Feedback will improve your story. Be open to new ideas and suggestions on how to communicate your thoughts. While your core idea, architecture, and story make perfect sense to you, other people will have alternate approaches for making the pitch. Their ideas might be better than yours. It would be a shame to exclude those thoughts from your pitch. They might offer pieces of information that make your pitch more compelling. They could identify major roadblocks that could derail your recommendation. They may know ways to get around barriers to your idea's implementation. Their thoughts could improve your pitch's quality and make its execution more successful. Isn't that the goal of all this hard work? Accept their feedback for what it is—assistance that makes you more successful. If they didn't care about your idea, they wouldn't take time out of their busy schedule to provide input.

You have the power of the pen. Just because someone suggests you include something in your pitch, it doesn't mean you have to. Remember, you can choose to include or exclude others' thoughts and advice. You're the one who has to be comfortable with the final pitch. If you think someone has made a great suggestion, by all means, include it. If you find their point to be irrelevant, ignore it. But remember, they thought the point was important enough to bring up. If you exclude someone's suggestion, be prepared to explain why you left that information out of your pitch.

The one exception to this guidance is the situation where someone else has the power of the pen. You may find yourself in situations where you're preparing a pitch for someone else to present. Many times you'll experience this with your boss or other senior stakeholders you create documents for. In those situations, the person making the pitch gets to dictate what's included or excluded. After all, they're the one on the podium staking their reputation on the recommendation. They have to be comfortable with the information in their pitch. If they tell you to include something you don't believe should be included, explain your rationale to try to sway them, but respect their final decision.

Have *Discussions*

When you're ready to start your discussions, create a stakeholder list. Identify as many people or groups who will be affected by your recommendation as you can. Remember to think broadly about who your stakeholders might be. Include groups like Operations, HR, Finance, IT, Legal, Regulatory, Sales, Marketing, adjacent business units, and other functional areas. Add peers from other departments. Perhaps include customers. Most important, add your nemesis. There are specific reasons for including these groups or individuals. What follows is the basic rationale for getting perspectives from each one.

Operations can provide perspectives on your idea's frontline impact. They'll tell you if your recommendation will help or harm day-to-day operations. Operations can point out secondary impacts arising from your recommendation. They could identify a need to budget for training for frontline associates. They might explain system or process impacts you haven't considered. Many times, Operations is the group that has to execute your idea. Their support is a major determinant of your rec-ommendation's success or failure.

Human Resources can let you know if your pitch will have unintended personnel consequences. They could point out your idea will require hiring or firing people, and they can then share the expected timelines and costs related to those actions. HR could explain your idea's compensation and bonus impacts. They might identify labor rules that are barriers to your idea's execution. There are many deal breakers HR will be aware of. Making a recommendation without their input is a risky proposition.

Finance controls the budget and has input into evaluating the financial case for your pitch. You might have the greatest idea ever, but if there's no budget available to pay for it, the idea isn't worth the paper the business case is written on. You should know up front if there will be funds available to pursue your idea. If there aren't, either figure out how you'll get approval for funding, or shelve your idea and explore other opportunities. Have Finance review the assumptions you're making and the analyses you plan to conduct. Ensure they're satisfied with the analytical method you're proposing and the rigor of your approach. Later on in the process, circle back with Finance and have them review your analytical results to ensure they're bought into your conclusions.

Information Technology knows the systems required for your idea's implementation. They know what data is available for you to conduct your analyses. IT should know what the current project prioritization list looks like. That knowledge can show you where your rec-ommendation stacks up relative to other ideas that have already been approved. Those projects ahead of your idea will drive how quickly your idea gets implemented. Seek IT's perspectives on system challenges, how you can overcome system limitations, and timelines required for implementing your idea.

Legal and Regulatory groups will point out laws and regulations governing how your idea gets implemented. I've seen cases where someone failed to speak with Legal before making their final recommendation. In the final steering committee meeting, this individual pitched their idea only to be informed by the attorney in the room that the idea was against the law. Needless to say, the pitch wasn't approved, and the individual making it looked quite foolish. Ask the Legal and Regulatory teams what rules are in place that could impact your recommendation before you run off and conduct analysis.

Sales and Marketing can explain prior efforts similar to your idea as well as tell you what the customer impacts might be if your idea is implemented. If your recommendation will impact customers in any way, the Sales and Marketing teams will be influential players with substantial input into your pitch's approval. Sales and Marketing have a wealth of customer research and data you can incorporate into your pitch rather than conducting time consuming analyses from scratch. Remember, this method is about efficiency and there are few approaches more efficient than using analysis that already exists.

Adjacent teams working upstream or downstream from you or teams you support will identify secondary effects you might not appreciate. For example, if your recommendation reduces costs in Operations, teams in Customer Service or Sales will want to know that. They might be able to offer better prices or discounts to customers because there's more margin available for making such offers. Look to these teams to point out your idea's unintended consequences. A change you make that improves customer retention could cause staffing issues for your customer service organization. Why? If you're keeping more customers, the customer service team will need enough associates to service those customers. If you don't tell them about your idea being implemented, they might find themselves short-staffed.

Peers from other teams provide a unique perspective because they don't *have* a perspective on your work. When you share your idea with someone who's unfamiliar with the context or the recommendation, they can identify gaps in logic. You might be assuming knowledge on the part of your audience. If the audience doesn't have the background, your pitch could fall apart. It's difficult for you to see these gaps because your personal knowledge fills them in. A peer without context will have an easier time pointing out these gaps. Choose a peer who won't be impacted by your recommendation. This creates a situation where they don't have an agenda and can be more objective in the feedback they provide. If your pitch is going to positively affect them, they might miss opportunities to be critical of your idea. They might be too harsh on your recommendation in an effort to derail it if your idea is going to affect them negatively. Their objectivity should result in them providing a more balanced perspective.

Customers are easy to forget if you're not on a team with direct customer interaction. Oftentimes your customers are two or three levels removed from your daily work. Ignoring your idea's impact on customers is a big mistake you must avoid. Imagine recommending something like automating a process to save money only to find out customers hate the automated process and, as a result, stop buying your company's products. The small savings gained by your idea could be dwarfed by the lost sales it causes. Always seek to understand your recommendation's customer impacts, no matter how far removed you might feel from the customer.

Your nemesis is the person who is most likely to oppose your recommendation. They may have goals that compete with yours. Your pitch could create risk for a major initiative they're pursuing. You may be competing for the same resources and if your idea is approved, their idea won't be. Heck, they may dislike you on a personal level. Whatever the reason, this person often wants to see your idea fail. At the very least, they're critical of your recommendation. They're the most important person for you to seek out for their concerns. Instead of avoiding your nemesis because you know the conversation will be painful, get to them early in this syndication process. Understand their concerns so you have time to conduct analysis proving the merits of your idea far outweigh the concerns your nemesis might raise.

It's an ugly situation if you avoid your nemesis until your final presentation. In that meeting they'll bring up all the objections you would have known to expect had you spoken with them earlier in the process. When this happens, you erode support for your pitch because other stakeholders wonder why you didn't seek out your nemesis's concerns sooner. If you do seek out their concerns early and you're able to conduct the analysis proving the benefits of your pitch outweigh their concerns, your nemesis has little choice but to agree with your recommendation. Their grudging agreement is a powerful show of support for your pitch.

Key *Questions* to Ask

As you have your conversations with these stakeholders, there are a few questions to seek answers to. This isn't an exhaustive list of everything to ask, but it is a good starting point for those conversations. Consider the following:

- ✎ Is this idea big enough to excite people and get their support?
- ✎ Is the idea feasible? What are the hurdles to implementation?
- ✎ Are there operational, technological, regulatory, legal, people, customer, or competitive impacts to consider?
- ✎ What data do we have to support this idea? Have we done something similar in the past?
- ✎ What are the goals of the stakeholders involved? How does this idea move us closer to or further away from their goals?
- ✎ What holes exist in my thinking? Who can fill them in?
- ✎ What are the decision maker's buttons? How should I push them?

These questions can prevent wasted effort. The first one on the list is my personal favorite. I worked for a great leader who taught me the importance of answering that question. I tend to have new ideas every day and I get excited about pursuing them. When I worked for Paul, there were many times I had what I thought was a great idea. In my excitement I would rush into his office and start sharing my idea. Before I could get three sentences into my pitch, Paul would hold up his hand in a motion for me to stop talking. He would then ask, "How many zeroes?" I'd reply, "Okay," and leave his office. The question he was asking was if there were enough zeroes after the first digit of my idea's financial impact for him to be excited about the idea. If the idea wasn't worth at least $100,000 in impact, it wasn't worth pursuing because it would never be high enough on the prioritization list to be implemented. That one question saved me countless hours of analyzing ideas that would never be executed.

This step can be time consuming. You'll have many meetings about your idea. You'll gather a great deal of input to further improve your idea and build support for your final pitch. Realize you'll be getting all this input no matter what. It's a question of whether you get the input and build support before or after you make your pitch. If you get input before the approval meeting, you'll identify the barriers to your idea. You can then come up with ways around those barriers or have the analysis proving the benefits of your idea outweigh the costs of those barriers. You'll build support from the stakeholder groups who have a voice in the final approval decision. If you wait until after your approval meeting to have all these conversations, your idea will likely be disapproved, and you'll have to have all these conversations anyway. Those conversations will be more uncomfortable when people ask, "Why didn't you ask for my perspective before you shared your recommendation?" You're better off getting these perspectives earlier in the structured thought process. Early syndication prevents wasted effort and enables you to build support for your pitch before the approval meeting.

10

Go From Draft Story to *Final* Version

After you've identified the stakeholders you want input from and you're in the right frame of mind to get their thoughts, it's time to take your story from draft to final version. It's important to note that while syndicating your idea *begins* at this point in the process, it doesn't end here. From this point forward, you'll continue gathering stakeholder input in an effort to further refine your pitch and build buy-in for it.

The easiest way to illustrate how this technique works is with an example. What follows is the evolution of a story from concept to completion. You'll see it change based upon input from early stages of the syndication process all the way through the final recommendation. I acknowledge I haven't yet covered how to conduct your analysis, but the analyses below are straightforward enough that the example should make sense.

For this example, I'll draw from my personal experience. I was responsible for a program in which we offered discounts to customers to get them to remain loyal to our company. The program had been performing well until I took it over. After being in my role for about six weeks, we saw an alarming trend: the program was losing money. We knew if we recommended making changes to the program, we would have to get the approval of our executive vice president, who was several levels above me on the organization chart. She was the ultimate decision maker, but I couldn't go straight to her for approval. I would have to create my recommendation and build broad support before taking the recommendation to her.

The *Initial* Story

First, I worked with my boss and my team to generate an initial core idea. We started with this: *We should fix the program because we can reach our financial goal of generating $XMM in profits.* My boss supported that recommendation because he was accountable for reaching that financial goal. With that core idea in mind, the team and I elected to build a layer architecture because we knew our EVP wasn't familiar with the situation. The architecture resulted in the following initial story:

Our discount program used to perform well.

- X customers per year were offered discounts and Y% accepted the offers.
- Of those who accepted, we retained W% as customers for another six months.
- Every customer we retained represented $Z in incremental profits.

But the program's performance has declined recently.

- Customers we've retained are calling us more often, and they're now demanding discounts for longer periods of time.
- Those call costs plus the extended discounts mean they're now unprofitable customers.
- The loss we're experiencing with each customer is $A per year, which means we're on track to lose $BMM over the next twelve months.

We should change the discount program rules for some segments because we'll reduce call volumes by C% and increase profits by $DMM this year.

- Change the rules for some segments.
- Call volumes will decrease by C%.
- Profits will increase by $DMM.

Gather *Additional* Perspectives and Data

After getting my boss's approval of the initial story, we took the story to IT. They said we could make the changes but rewriting the system rules would cost about $100,000. We also spoke with our director—my boss's boss. He mentioned our EVP would want to know the sales impact of these changes and which segments we would target for the changes. Our call center manager told us to remember short-term call cost increases because of the rule changes. After getting all that input, our story changed. On the next page is the revised story. I've italicized the points that changed.

●◆

We added the technology cost estimates, hypothesized as to which segments to target, changed from call volumes to call costs, and added the sales impact of the changes. Feedback from our stakeholders led to important changes to our story. We then conducted preliminary analysis and filled in several variables. One analysis indicated we should focus on segments 1, 3, and 4 instead of segments 1 and 2. Armed with those numbers, we brought our story to our vice president. He suggested we leave out the points about net call costs because they weren't as important as profits and sales.

Our discount program used to perform well.

- X customers per year were offered discounts and Y% accepted the offers.

- Of those who accepted, we retained W% as customers for another six months.

- Every customer we retained represented $Z in incremental profits *and $V in sales.*

But the program's performance has declined recently.

- Customers we've retained are calling us more often, and they're now demanding discounts for longer periods of time.

- Those call costs plus the extended discounts mean they're now unprofitable customers.

- The loss we're experiencing with each customer is $A per year, which means we're on track to lose $BMM over the next twelve months.

- *Sales for these segments have declined by $E which will result in a sales decrease of $FMM in the next twelve months.*

We should change the discount program rules for *segments 1 and 2* because we'll reduce *net* call *costs* by C%, increase profits by $DMM *and sales by $GMM* this year.

- Change the rules for *segments 1 and 2, which will cost $100,000.*

- *Net* call *costs* will decrease by C%.

- Profits will increase by $DMM.

- *Sales will increase by $GMM this year.*

Meeting With Our Nemesis

After making those modifications, we set up a time with our senior vice president. By the time we spoke with him, we had completed our analyses and turned our story into a near-final presentation. Our meeting with him lasted two hours. He asked detailed questions about all our analyses. He probed for clarity on the segmentation analysis. He explored the technology changes we were proposing and the timeline for completing them. His questions went on forever. Our SVP was our nemesis. He wasn't necessarily against our idea, but he was critical of our analyses and conclusions. After two hours of explanation, he said he understood and supported the recommendation. He suggested we cover sales before discussing profits because our EVP had been showing more interest in sales lately.

The *Final* Pitch

We based our presentation to our EVP upon the following story:

Our discount program used to perform well.

- *243,500* customers per year were offered discounts and *43%* accepted the offers.
- Of those who accepted, we retained *87%* as customers for another six months.
- Every customer we retained represented *$1,423 in sales and $167 in incremental profits.*

But the program's performance has declined recently.

- Customers we've retained are now demanding discounts for longer periods of time.
- Those extended discounts mean they're now unprofitable customers.
- *Sales for segments 1, 3, and 4 have declined by $327 per customer, which will result in a sales decrease of $8.9MM in the next twelve months.*
- *The loss we're experiencing with each customer is $264 per year, which means we're on track to lose $7.2MM over the next twelve months.*

We should change the discount program rules for *segments 1, 3, and 4* because we'll increase *sales by $4.5MM and profits by $3.6MM* this year.

- Change the *discount* rules for *segments 1, 3 and 4, which will cost $100,000 for technology changes.*
- *Sales will increase by $4.5MM this year.*
- *Profits will increase by $3.6MM this year.*

When we presented our findings to our EVP, the conversation flowed. There was a natural progression from our "Background" section to our "What's Changed" section. Our core idea made sense to her, and she found the impact on sales and profits compelling. After we presented the idea, she asked our SVP, VP, and the IT representative in the room what they thought. All three supported the recommendation. We received immediate approval for the IT changes and left the room with a signed business case.

All told, the conversation took thirty minutes. We had invested several hours in conversations with stakeholders before the meeting. Those investments paid off. Based upon the feedback we received, we focused on the right analyses and shared the information in a sequence that made sense. We eliminated several distractions, like net call costs, and emphasized the metrics our EVP cared about—sales and profits.

If we had gone into the final meeting without having received all the feedback that came in the story refinement process, our presentation would not have gone as well. We might have confused our EVP. Even worse, our SVP would have asked all his probing questions. Given our time slot was a short thirty minutes, his questions could have derailed the meeting. He would have asked for a follow-up meeting to get in-depth answers to his questions. We would have spent the two hours with him *after* meeting with our EVP. She could have perceived his questions as a lack of support for our idea. Even worse, we would have wasted thirty minutes of our EVP's time because we weren't able to drive to a decision.

We avoided all these issues by getting feedback throughout the structured thought process. We got basic guidance at the core idea step, more input at the story step, additional perspectives during the analysis steps, and further refinement right before the final presentation step. All that feedback made our recommendation better and resulted in approval the first time we made our pitch. Getting on stakeholder calendars and making time for all these conversations was worth the effort.

Sometimes you won't be able to get on a stakeholder's calendar because they're busy. In other situations you won't have enough time to get to all the stakeholders you want input from. Time is always a limited commodity. Fortunately, both of these obstacles can be overcome.

When *Stakeholders* Are Too Busy to Speak With You

For situations where it's difficult to get on the stakeholder's calendar, see if you can find a proxy for their perspective. Try speaking with one of the stakeholder's direct reports or team members. They'll be familiar with how the stakeholder thinks, and they'll know what the stakeholder's concerns are. While their perspectives won't exactly reflect the stakeholder's, they should be able to cover the most important points for you. You can also speak with other people who have presented to that stakeholder recently. Ask them what kinds of questions the stakeholder asked. If your colleague presented to the stakeholder a few weeks ago and they were asked ten questions about the sales impact of their idea, there's a good chance you'll receive similar questions.

If you're unable to speak with a stakeholder's team members and you don't know anyone who has presented to that stakeholder, there are other ways to figure out what they'll want you to cover. Look at their title and job description. If they're the call center manager, they're going to want to know the impacts on call center operations. If they're the VP of Marketing, you'll probably be asked to explain how the idea should be marketed to customers. Ask yourself, "If I were this stakeholder, what would I be concerned about?" Their job description is a great starting point. Take a look at their LinkedIn profile for clues about their interests and biases. While they may be a VP of Compliance now, if they had prior roles in Legal and Finance, you can expect questions on legal or finance topics. Do your detective work to get inside their minds.

In addition to thinking about their interests, see if you can get a copy of your stakeholder's personal or team goals. If their top three goals have to do with operational efficiency, it's a solid bet they'll ask you about your idea's operational impacts. If their team has a strategic plan or presentations explaining the team's responsibilities, read them. Those documents will highlight their goals, key metrics, top projects, and threats and opportunities they face. You should know if your project is going to be competing for the same resources as the top project in your stakeholder's strategic plan. If that's the case, expect them to be resistant to your pitch because it could negatively impact their results. The more information you have about a stakeholder, the better you'll be able to predict and address their concerns. Don't let their full calendar stop you from incorporating their perspectives.

When *You* Are Too Busy to Speak With Stakeholders

Deadlines can be tight, and you'll find yourself in situations where you don't have enough time to speak with all the stakeholders you'd like to speak with. While you'd love to incorporate all their thoughts and refine your story accordingly, your schedule doesn't afford you the luxury of meeting with everyone to get their perspectives. You have two choices in this situation: you can either ask for a deadline extension, or you can prioritize your stakeholders and speak with the most important ones. Since the former is unlikely, let's focus on the latter.

Start by making your stakeholder list. Be comprehensive and include all the groups that will be impacted by your recommendation. Write down your best guess as to what their points of support, concern, and opposition could be. Look at your pitch from their perspective. Discuss your list with a teammate if you have time. Have them add their thoughts to round out the perspective. Look at the list for common themes and major concerns and write those items down. This is your list of major issues to address in your final presentation. Next, prioritize your issue list. Put the biggest issues to resolve at the top of the list. As you work through the rest of the process, gather information and conduct analyses designed to address these issues. By focusing on themes and common issues, you can address the concerns of multiple stakeholders through a few analyses.

Next, list the names of the stakeholders who will be the most resistant or who can be the most influential in the approval process. These are the people to speak with in your limited time. Get on their calendars if possible. If you don't have time for a meeting, send them your draft story via email. Be clear about the feedback you want from them. Direct them to comment on specific points in your story or to address large concerns you think they might have. Ask them to reply via email, call, or meet with you to discuss the issues. If the issue is of big enough concern for them, they'll make the time to speak with you. Do the best you can to address these issues in your final pitch to the extent you have time to do the required analysis.

If after you exhaust all those options you still have unresolved issues and concerns, include them in your pitch in an "Open Issues" page near the end of your presentation. List the major unresolved issues, whom you intend to resolve them with, and when you expect to have resolution completed. By acknowledging the issues are open, you blunt the attacks of people who might oppose your pitch because you haven't addressed their concern. When you have this list of open issues, you can ask for conditional approval of your pitch pending the positive resolution of the items on your list. With approval in hand, you're able to proceed with your idea as soon as you resolve everything on the list and you don't have to go back to your decision makers for another conversation. Once you've resolved the issues, send an email to your decision makers to let them know all the issues have been addressed and you're proceeding with the idea per their prior approval. That's a more efficient approach than going back to them and presenting your pitch a second time.

The discussion and refinement process can be lengthy and exhausting, but your end product will be bulletproof.

This step requires you to spend substantial amounts of time with your stakeholders before the final pitch. If you skip getting their input and wait until the final presentation, you'll likely find yourself getting their input anyway—only it'll be after your pitch didn't go as well as it could have gone.

Identify the *Required* Facts

The basis for a compelling pitch is a solid fact base. You'll need proof for every point you make in your story. What I find most interesting about the structured thought process is the amount of thought that goes into a pitch before you even begin gathering data. Here we are, eleven chapters into the method before we're discussing gathering facts. This is why the method is efficient. You're doing your thinking before rushing off and conducting time-consuming analysis and research. All that thinking focuses you on gathering facts that will make your case stronger versus gathering facts because they're interesting.

You may find this notion of not gathering data until this late in the process unrealistic. Do not mistake the length of the chapters preceding this as a proxy for the amount of time you'll spend on the process. I've been in situations where we went from question to core idea to architecture in two days. We wrote the story and syndicated it in two days. We were in analysis mode on day five of the project. In other situations, you'll already have significant amounts of background analysis complete before you even start a project using the structured thought process. Many pitches you'll make will be related to your everyday work. You can use existing analysis to form your preliminary perspectives as you craft your core idea and your architecture. The broader takeaway is you need to think about structuring your pitch before conducting substantive analysis.

Whether you realize it or not, you've already identified the facts you need to gather and the analyses you need to conduct. You did this when you created your architecture. Previously, I mentioned you would build your architecture from the top down and then "prove" your core idea from the bottom up. The core idea drove your architecture's structure and content. The bullet points in your architecture will drive the analyses you use to support your case. Those analyses will prove or disprove the points you've made in your architecture. If the analyses prove the case, you'll proceed with your recommendation. If they disprove elements of your architecture, you'll iterate and modify your architecture—and even your core idea—until all the points in your pitch are fully supported by facts.

Choose Your *Analyses*

You'll need facts and analysis to support every point in your architecture. Sometimes the support will be a simple analysis, a page with customer quotes, a process diagram, or any set of facts that lead to your conclusion. Other times this will require several rigorous analyses to prove the point. The point you're trying to prove will dictate which facts to gather and which analyses to conduct. Let's look at how the architecture in Figure 6.4 (p. 98) dictates the analyses that need to be conducted. For each point in the architecture, I've suggested analyses that could be used to support the point.

Buy a new dialer

↪ Our dialer is old and keeps breaking down.

Analysis: timeline explaining the history of when the dialer was put into service.

Analysis: error and downtime reporting for the dialer showing the frequency of breakdowns and the amount of downtime for the last six months.

↪ There are newer and better dialers on the market.

Analysis: list of the top three dialers on the market with an explanation of their main features and functionality compared to our current dialer's functionality.

↪ A better, more reliable dialer will improve our collections performance.

Analysis: historical collections performance of our current dialer compared to estimated collections performance with a new dialer.

Analysis: estimated lost collections dollars attributable to the errors and downtimes of our current dialer for the last six months.

Buy from vendor ABC

☞ Vendor ABC sells high-quality dialers.

Analysis: assessment of Vendor ABC's top dialers. The analysis includes features and functionality as well as any industry benchmarking of ABC's dialers versus competitor dialers.

☞ Vendor ABC has competitive pricing.

Analysis: price list for Vendor ABC's dialers compared to the prices of other comparable dialers in the market.

☞ Only one other vendor's products are approved by our IT group, Vendor DEF.

Analysis: list of the top dialer manufacturers including ABC and DEF and their approval status with IT. If a manufacturer is not approved, include the reason why.

☞ Vendor DEF's product is inferior to vendor ABC's.

Analysis: side-by-side comparison of DEF's top products compared to ABC's top products. Key evaluation dimensions should include the metrics most important to the collections organization like speed, reliability, accuracy, and so on.

Reduce losses

☞ Our losses have increased by \$ZMM this year.

Analysis: show historical losses for the last three years and highlight the increase of \$ZMM this year.

☞ A new dialer could deliver loss reduction of \$XMM per year.

Analysis: show expected future loss reduction attributable to a new dialer versus continuing with the existing dialer status quo.

Every analysis is linked to a point from the architecture. All told, it's eleven analyses. There are dozens of other analyses that *could* be conducted but they don't *need* to be conducted. If these eleven analyses prove the points they're designed to prove, then those points hold as true. If those points hold true, the three columns hold true. If the columns hold true, the core idea *We should buy a new dialer from Vendor ABC to reduce our losses by \$XMM per year* is proven. This is what I mean by building from the top down then proving from the bottom up.

This approach applies to layer architectures too. Every point in the architecture must be supported by facts. The points themselves indicate which analyses to conduct. Here's how you might define analyses for a layer approach using Figure 7.1 (p. 113) as an example.

Background

☞ Our team has twenty-seven personnel who conduct document processing activities.

We've been at that staffing level for the last four years.

Analysis: bar chart showing staffing levels for the last four years.

↝ Document processing volumes have been steadily increasing over that time period, but we've been able to meet demand and achieve our service level requirements.

Analysis: line graph showing document processing volumes and how they've increased for the last four years.

Analysis: bar chart showing the team meeting or exceeding service level requirements for the last four years.

↝ Our team's performance is measured by service level agreements, and we consistently meet our goals. When we meet our goals, the company does well. If we fail to meet goals, company sales and profit performance suffer.

Analysis: chart showing service levels correlated with company sales and profit performance over the last four years.

What's changed

↝ Document processing volumes are continuing to increase and we're forecasting a personnel shortage for next year

Analysis: line chart showing current and projected document processing volumes.

Analysis: staffing required to meet service levels for increased document-processing volumes. Analysis should highlight the magnitude of the personnel shortage for next year.

☞ If we have a personnel shortage, we won't be able to achieve our service level goals, and company performance will suffer in the form of lower sales and profits.

Analysis: forecasted service levels if staffing is not increased but document processing volumes increase as projected.

Analysis: expected sales and profit performance based upon correlation between short-staffed service levels and company financial metrics.

Core idea

☞ We should hire five new team members because we'll be able to meet increased processing demands and help the company achieve its sales and profit goals.

Analysis: calculate the staffing gap and show how five personnel will be sufficient to fill the expected gap.

Analysis: show projected future service levels with the incremental five personnel given the expected document processing volume increase.

Analysis: expected sales and profit performance based upon correlation between fully-staffed service levels and company financial metrics.

This is another situation where eleven analyses would be sufficient to support the recommendation. Every analysis on the list is necessary. If any analyses were left out, the argument would be weaker, if not entirely invalidated.

If the analyses all play out as expected, those results should be enough to get the pitch approved.

Necessary and *Sufficient* Analysis

Choosing analyses based upon every point in your architecture ensures you cover the necessary facts. Without those analyses, that particular point in your architecture won't be supported. An unsupported point can cause your entire argument to collapse. Conversely, if you conduct extra analyses unrelated to proving a point, those analyses aren't necessary. This is one way you can eliminate wasted effort. Redundant and irrelevant analyses do nothing more than frustrate your audience. If the analysis isn't conducted to support a point in the architecture, you don't need it and you shouldn't be wasting your time on it. If you include excessive analysis to support a point, your audience will grow weary of those facts because they've already received enough information to consider the point proven. Focusing on the necessary facts will save you time and effort. That focus will make your meetings shorter and more productive. Let your architecture govern your analytical efforts.

You can use your architecture to manage stakeholder requests for additional analysis. We've all received requests to conduct irrelevant analysis. Unfortunately, when this happens, the only choices we have are to capitulate and do the analysis, even though we know it's a waste of time or argue with our stakeholder about why we don't need to do the work. In the former scenario, we're wasting time and energy. In the latter, we can be perceived as uncooperative, insubordinate, lazy, or frustrating. Without a clear rationale for not doing the work, those arguments come across as whining and complaining.

If you have an architecture, you can push back on stakeholders in a logical way. If your stakeholder asks you to perform an analysis you think is irrelevant, pull out your architecture. If they've already bought into your architecture, this is a powerful technique. By agreeing with your pitch's logic, they've given you an effective way to ask them how the analysis fits into proving the case. One of two things will happen: they'll either explain how the requested analysis contributes to proving the case, or they'll realize the analysis isn't necessary to proving the case. In the first situation, include their requested analysis in your architecture. In the second case, they should be willing to abandon the analysis because they see why it's irrelevant.

In addition to making sure your analyses are necessary, the analysis you conduct has to be sufficient to prove your case. Weak analysis results in a weak argument. You need to have enough data to convince your audience your recommendation is correct. If you're trying to convince your audience to spend tens of thousands of dollars to launch a new product, you'll need compelling evidence. If your analysis consists of quotes from fifteen people saying they love your product, that's not sufficient for making your case. If you had market-research data from 15,000 consumers that made the same point, that would be sufficient. This is a "burden of proof" point. You need to have sufficient data to get a skeptical audience to agree with your recommendation. It's easy to get people who support your pitch to go along with less rigorous data, but they aren't the people you need to win over. You need to have facts that will sway your detractors and your nemesis from a position of resistance to one of support. Sufficient data is the way to make that shift happen.

Using your architecture to drive your analytical efforts is an efficient and effective way to ensure you have all the right information you need to prove your case. The analytical plan you execute will be focused on bringing the right data, and only the right data, to your final pitch meeting.

12

Prove and *Disprove* Hypotheses

Up to this point in the structured thought process, you've had little or no data. You've been operating purely on hypotheses. Once you've identified the analyses to conduct to prove your case, it's time to run the numbers. Those analyses will either prove or disprove your hypotheses. Many times, the analysis will prove the hypotheses in your architecture. Sometimes analysis will disprove them. When you conduct analysis, be open to disproving your initial hypotheses. The structured thought process is about getting to the right answer, not about proving your initial hypotheses were correct. Analytical rigor is required if you want to deliver a pitch that will convince even your most skeptical critics.

If your hypotheses are proven, your core idea will be proven and you'll move your idea forward in the structured thought process. If the hypotheses are disproven, you'll assess how the analysis changes your recommendation. In some cases, the changes to your story will be subtle. In others, your entire core idea will change. The magnitude of those changes depends upon which hypotheses are disproven and how important they are to making your case.

Proving Hypotheses and Avoiding Pitfalls

The best-case scenario you can hope for is the analysis you perform proves all your hypotheses. In those situations, your entire architecture and story will remain intact and your core idea will become your final recommendation. Oftentimes, you'll find yourself in this situation. This happens because you're already familiar with the subject matter at hand. If you've been in your role or profession for several years, you've accumulated a wealth of knowledge about the way things work. You have a large "database" of information filled with your prior experience. Recall that hypotheses are best guesses as to what the correct answer is. Those guesses are based upon a gut reaction for the solution to the problem. Gut reactions are derived from your instinct, experience, and knowledge of a situation. The deeper your experience in a field, the more likely it is your gut reactions will be correct.

While it's great to have experience and prove your hypotheses are correct, that same experience carries risk with it. Confirmation bias—the tendency to look for or interpret information in a way that confirms your pre-conceived ideas—is the biggest risk you face when using a hypothesis-driven approach like the structured thought process. No one wants to be wrong, so it's easy to fall into the trap of thinking disproving your hypothesis means you made a mistake. That fear of being wrong can lead you to wear blinders when you're conducting analysis. You might ignore or dismiss facts contrary to your hypothesis. You might only look for data that proves you're correct, which can then skew your analytical results. Before you know it, you're making a case based upon incorrect information.

The end result of succumbing to confirmation bias is you'll present a recommendation with flawed supporting data. If your audience picks up on your bias, they'll call you out on it, and you'll have to go back and redo your work without the blinders on. If they don't notice your bias and they approve your recommendation, you'll be implementing an idea that could be harmful to your organization. Neither one of those outcomes is acceptable.

To avoid confirmation bias, enlist the aid of others. Get independent views of your analysis, and ask people if you're missing anything. I know leaders who encourage their team members to try to prove them wrong with additional analysis. Their thinking is if no one on their team can prove their recommendation is wrong, then the answer they've arrived at is right. It takes courage to put yourself out there like that and ask your team to prove you're wrong. But if you focus on the objective of getting to the right answer and see this as a way to ensure you do, it's easier to take this approach.

Involving your nemesis is another check to prevent confirmation bias. If anyone is looking for flaws in your work, they are. They'll spot situations where you've ignored data that's counter to your hypothesis. They'll point out when your interpretation of the facts is skewed in favor of proving you're right. While their challenges can be frustrating, your nemesis can prevent you from making the big mistake of implementing a flawed recommendation.

Assuming you're able to avoid confirmation bias pitfalls, beware of another trap: analysis paralysis. Many people have the mistaken belief that if some data is good, more data is better, and excessive amounts of data is best. In reality, all that extra analysis is wasted time and effort. Once you have enough analysis to prove your point, stop doing analysis! All you're doing is spending time on something that won't generate incremental benefits.

Excessive analysis increases the risk of upsetting your audience. The more data you share with them, the longer the meeting ends up being. If they're supportive of your answer after four analyses and you insist on showing them ten more analyses they understand but don't need, they'll grow frustrated. Those feelings won't help you get your pitch approved! If they're confused by the irrelevant or redundant analyses you're sharing, the likelihood of getting your pitch approved in the meeting will plummet. Know when enough analysis is enough.

The flip side of analysis paralysis is insufficient or weak analysis. Your facts must support the hypothesis enough to convince others the hypothesis is true. For example, if your hypothesis states customers will buy 5,000 units of your new product in the first month it's released, you'll need rigorous analysis to make your case. If the analysis you use to support this hypothesis is two prospective customers you met in a store said they would buy the product immediately, that's likely insufficient evidence to prove your case. You would need deeper market projections with statistically significant data to make a convincing argument. If you're not sure if your evidence is compelling enough to convince your audience, ask your nemesis what they think about the conclusions you're drawing based upon the data. If your nemesis is convinced by your analysis, it's likely others who are less skeptical will be convinced too.

If your analyses support all the hypotheses from your architecture and your story, nothing about your recommendation should change. Rather than share a lengthy example to demonstrate that point, I'll simply encourage you to focus on avoiding the pitfalls that could lead you to make a case based upon flawed analysis. Once you've documented all your analyses and linked them to each hypothesis in your story, you're ready to finalize your recommendation—which I'll cover in the next chapter.

Disproving Hypotheses

The data don't always do what you want the data to do. Sometimes you'll conduct analyses and come to the conclusion your hypothesis is disproven. That's a good outcome. Be open to having a hypothesis disproven. When you disprove a hypothesis, you've learned something new. The conventional wisdom may point to a hypothesis stating you should go north but the analysis shows going north is a bad idea. That analysis indicates going south is a better course of action. That new information is an insight that can create an advantage for you in the market. If your competitors still *believe* they should move north but you *know* it's better to move south, you're one step ahead of them because you disproved the initial hypothesis.

When disproving hypotheses, you'll conduct your analysis the same way you did when you proved hypotheses. Evaluate each hypothesis and supporting point in your architecture and story. Conduct the analysis with an eye toward proving or disproving each individual point. Once you've proven or disproven a point, document your results and move on to proving or disproving the next point. Before you begin your next analysis, ask yourself if the analysis you completed invalidates your entire argument. If it does, there's no need for additional analysis to prove or disprove the other points of your story. If the analysis doesn't invalidate the argument, continue proving or disproving each individual hypothesis and, after you've evaluated each one, synthesize your results for the entire story.

When disproving hypotheses, beware of the same pitfalls of confirmation bias and analysis paralysis. If you're trying to disprove someone else's hypotheses, you still face the same risk of confirmation bias. You might only look at data disproving the hypothesis and ignore data supporting it. As far as analysis paralysis goes, there's a higher risk of succumbing to that dynamic when disproving hypotheses. This happens because you want to be *absolutely sure* your hypothesis is disproven, therefore you tend to do more analysis than needed to support your position. Once you've disproven the hypothesis, stop doing analysis!

After you've conducted all your analysis, assess the impact of the hypotheses you disproved. If the ones you disproved are minor points, your overarching core idea might still hold true, but the way you support it might change. If you disproved something major, your entire core idea could change. This step of proving and disproving hypotheses is one where you might iterate multiple times. Continue iterating until *all* the points in your architecture are proven, or until you declare the entire argument invalid and move on to your next best idea as your core idea. When that happens, you'll start the entire structured thought process over again to prove your new hypothesis.

Example: Disproving Hypotheses While Keeping Your Core Idea

Sometimes you'll disprove elements of your story but the core idea will remain mostly intact. Here's one such scenario. Using Figure 6.4 (p. 98) and the analyses tied to each hypothesis, I've documented the results of each analysis and indicated whether the hypothesis was proven or not. Recall our core idea was: *We should buy a new dialer from Vendor ABC to reduce our losses by $XMM per year.* Let's look at how the facts affect that core idea.

Buy a new dialer

- ✑ Our dialer is old and keeps breaking down.

  Proven: the dialer was put into service ten years ago.

  Proven: dialer error rates are up 18% and downtime increased 22% in the last six months.

- ✑ There are newer and better dialers on the market.

  Proven: the three top dialers in the market have far more features and better functionality than the dialer we're currently using.

- ✑ A better, more reliable dialer will improve our collections performance.

  Proven: a new dialer will result in 16% better collections performance.

  Proven: our current dialer's errors and downtimes cost us $1.2MM in lost collections dollars in the last six months.

Buy from Vendor ABC

- ✑ Vendor ABC sells high-quality dialers.

  Proven (mostly): Vendor ABC's dialers have *equal* or better functionality versus all competitor dialers.

- ✑ Vendor ABC has competitive pricing.

  Disproven: Vendor ABC's dialers are on average 9% more expensive than comparable dialers and 11% more expensive than Vendor DEF's dialers.

- ✑ Only one other vendor's products are approved by our IT group, Vendor DEF.

> *Proven:* Vendors ABC and DEF are both on the IT-approved list.

☞ Vendor DEF's product is inferior to Vendor ABC's.

> **Disproven**: Vendor DEF's top products are *on par* with all features and functionality of Vendor ABC's top products.

Reduce losses

☞ Our losses have increased by $ZMM this year.

> *Proven:* losses have increased by $6.2MM this year.

☞ A new dialer could deliver loss reduction of $XMM per year.

> *Proven:* a new dialer will reduce losses by $4.8MM versus continuing with the existing dialer status quo.

The majority of the hypotheses are proven. We indeed need to buy a new dialer, and buying one will improve our financial performance. But we disproved two hypotheses. First, Vendor ABC's dialers are mostly superior to other competitive offerings, but they're on par with Vendor DEF. Second, Vendor ABC's products are 11% more expensive than Vendor DEF's. Based upon those two points and the fact that Vendor DEF is already an IT-approved vendor, we would modify our core idea from "We should buy a new dialer from *Vendor ABC* to reduce our losses by $4.8MM per year" to "We should buy a new dialer from *Vendor DEF* to reduce our losses by $4.8MM per year." Vendor DEF's feature parity and more competitive pricing make it a better choice than buying from Vendor ABC.

This is a case where disproving hypotheses led us to a better answer. Had we succumbed to confirmation bias and skewed the case in favor of Vendor ABC, we would be overpaying for our new dialer with no incremental performance benefits. While most of the story remained intact, the vendor choice recommendation switched based upon disproving the hypotheses related to functionality and cost. When you disprove hypotheses in your story, modify the final story and core idea accordingly.

Example: Disproving Hypotheses and Changing Your Core Idea

Many times, you'll face situations where disproving hypotheses results in small modifications to your story like the example above. Occasionally, the hypotheses you disprove will result in a completely different recommendation. Let's look at the example in Figure 7.1 (p. 113) to see how this might play out. We're trying to prove the core idea *"We should hire five new team members because we'll be able to meet increased processing demands and help the company achieve its sales and profit goals."*

Background

⤷ Our team has twenty-seven personnel who conduct document processing activities. We've been at that staffing level for the last four years.

Proven: we've had twenty-seven people on the team for the last four years.

☞ Document processing volumes have been steadily increasing over that time period, but we've been able to meet demand and achieve our service level requirements.

Proven: document processing volumes have increased by 13% over the last four years.

Proven: our service levels have met or exceeded goals for the last four years.

☞ Our team's performance is measured by service level agreements, and we consistently meet our goals. When we meet our goals, the company does well. If we fail to meet goals, company sales and profit performance suffers.

Proven: service levels are directly correlated with company sales and profits.

What's changed

☞ Document processing volumes are continuing to increase and we're forecasting a personnel shortage for next year.

Disproven: because of recently installed automation we weren't aware of, document processing volumes are forecast to *decrease* by 32% next year and *decrease* 18% the year following. Volume isn't expected to increase in the years after that.

Disproven: based on the expected volume decrease, our team will be overstaffed by nine people next year and twelve people the year following.

∞ If we have a personnel shortage, we won't be
  able to achieve our service level goals, and
  company performance will suffer in the form
  of lower sales and profits.

  Disproven/irrelevant: we will not have a personnel shortage.

Our original core idea has been rendered void because
there's no way we should recommend adding staff when
volumes are decreasing and we're forecast to be overstaffed. The automation installation is a major piece of
new information we didn't have when we constructed our
architecture's first draft. That fact changes everything
about our recommendation. Armed with this new information, we can avoid all the work related to analyzing
service levels under a personnel-shortage situation. We
don't have to figure out what will happen to sales and
profits if we're understaffed because we now know we'll
have more than enough people to handle the volume.

Our focus should now turn to changing our core idea
to match the facts and figuring out how to support the
new core idea. We might change our core idea from *"We
should hire five new team members because we'll be able to
meet increased processing demands and help the company
achieve its sales and profit goals"* to *"We should reduce our
team's headcount by twelve people over the next two years because we can generate $XMM in cost savings while still meet-
ing document processing service levels."*

The iterative nature of the structured thought process will eventually get us to the correct recommendation. Disproving hypotheses is a trigger for iterating.
Once we've identified a possible new recommendation,
we should revise our architecture and story to include

hypotheses to support this new core idea. Next we would identify the analyses required to prove those hypotheses. This new core idea should be taken through the entire structured thought process until we've both proven the idea and made the new pitch, or we've disproven the idea and moved onto another recommendation.

Proving and disproving hypotheses with facts and analysis is what will make your case compelling. Using the structured thought process to focus on a select set of hypotheses derived from your architecture and story is what will make you more efficient. You'll do less junk analysis. By proving or disproving hypotheses, you'll iterate your way to the right answer that can be supported with a solid fact set. The hypothesis-driven approach enables you to take a guess up front then let the analysis guide you to the correct answer along the way, instead of obsessing about getting the right answer on the first attempt. Once you've iterated until all the points in your story are proven and your core idea has sufficient supporting evidence for you to consider it final, you're ready to transform your work into a final communication.

Finalize the Communication

At this stage of the structured thought process, you're done! You've been crafting your pitch all along without even realizing it. Think about it. You've defined a clear question and understand why it's important to solve the problem. You have a core idea that makes a compelling recommendation in a manner that resonates with your audience because you're pushing their button. Your architecture lays out your argument's logic and you've transformed your architecture into an easy-to-follow narrative in the form of your story. Stakeholders have provided their input, and you've adjusted your story accordingly. Incorporating their input makes your story more convincing and builds support for your pitch too. The analysis you've conducted based on your story proves your case. Now it's a matter of assembling this information into a final communication that pulls it all together.

The first decision to make is which communication format you'll use. You could choose to write a presentation, draft a memo, send an email, leave a voicemail, or create a business case. Your format choice should be based on the type of information you're presenting as well as your audience's preferred format. If your stakeholder prefers memos, write a memo. If they want a presentation, give them one. If they like emails and you leave a voicemail, your message won't go over as well as it could.

If you deliberately ignore their communication style preference, make sure you've got a good reason for doing so. You might have complex data best displayed in a presentation format. If your stakeholder loves voicemails, you'd be making a mistake by translating your complex data into a format that's not conducive to conveying that information. Imagine trying to explain a bar graph via voicemail. It doesn't work!

One principle to remember when drafting your final communication is more is not better, regardless of which communication format you use. Long presentations get painful after five pages when your audience sees they have thirty-five pages yet to go. People stop reading a memo after three pages. If someone has to scroll to read your entire email, it's too long. They'll delete your voicemail if they don't know what it's about in the first thirty seconds. In an age of 140 character tweets, text messages, and thirty second videos, your challenge is to keep someone's interest long enough to get them to approve your pitch. When you're not sure whether to include a detailed piece of information or not, err on the side of holding it back. Small details can always be shared in response to audience questions. If they don't ask about it, the information isn't important enough to share. Cramming as much detail as you can fit into your communication only serves to distract people away from your message. Stay focused on your story and the analyses or facts required to prove it. Any information beyond that is excessive.

Select a Communication *Format*

There are many ways to make your pitch. Choosing the right vehicle is often a matter of understanding the type of pitch you're making and the information required to make it. Each format has a reasonably standard set of elements required to make it effective. Here are common formats, guidance on when to use them, and core components of each:

Voicemail. This is one of the simplest communication vehicles. It should be reserved for the simplest of tasks. Use voicemail when the audience has full knowledge of the situation and you're providing them new information, requesting additional information from them, or asking them to make a quick decision. A good voicemail starts with a reminder of the issue you're calling about. Next, cover your call's purpose—updating, requesting information, or getting a decision—along with a timeline for action, if there is one. If while you're leaving your message your voicemail system's recorded voice comes on and says you have thirty seconds remaining to finish your message, that's a big warning indicator that you're talking too long. You're using the wrong communication format. You need to switch to a format more conducive to sharing more information.

Email. Use email when the audience has a solid understanding of the issue's context and when you're trying to get a quick decision or offer a short update. Email can be an effective communication tool when multiple people need to receive the same information because your email can be forwarded intact without changing the message. It's not an effective vehicle for sharing complex information or extensive amounts of data. A good email should contain a greeting, short context on the issue, a recommendation, a request for action, and a timeline. For update emails where no action is required, note that so your audience understands they don't need to do anything with the information other than absorb it.

Memo. This format is useful when the audience needs deeper context. It's a good choice when the information you're sharing requires more detailed explanation and you don't need to share complex visuals like graphs or images. If your organization has a standard memo format, use it. People are used to seeing information in that structure. If you change the structure, you could confuse them because you're making them change the way they've been conditioned to receive information. When you don't have to follow a standard format, the structured thought process makes drafting a memo easy. Take your story and convert it to memo format. If your audience isn't grounded on the subject, a layer-based story provides a good flow for your memo. If the audience is grounded, a column-based story should meet their information needs. Add detail to your memo as appropriate. This detail can take the form of data tables or simple embedded graphs. At the end of the memo, let your audience know what you want from them in terms of a decision or action required on their part. Remember to be explicit about any timing constraints or due dates for them to take action.

Presentation. This is the most common format for making a pitch. Use it when sharing complex data, concepts, or images. Most people are visual learners—approximately 65% by many accounts. They receive information most effectively in the form of a picture. Graphs, frameworks, diagrams, and images work well in these situations. A presentation enables you to convey large amounts of information in an easy to absorb format. A good presentation has a title page, an executive summary, the data and charts supporting your recommendation, a list of risks and opportunities, and clear next steps. Many presentations contain an appendix for more detailed supporting analyses that are important but not critical enough to include in the presentation's main body.

Presentations are common yet they seem to give people the most trouble when making a pitch. Fortunately the structured thought process enables you to navigate these challenges and create a compelling presentation. One of my favorite aspects of this method is the way it writes your presentation for you as you work your way through the structured thought process. Here's the logic behind that statement. The question scopes and defines the core idea. The core idea drives the architecture. The architecture defines the story. The architecture and story determine the analyses. Once the analyses prove your hypotheses, your presentation is done; it's but a matter of assembly. To illustrate how all your work so far comes together into a presentation, see Figure 13.1 which lays out the pages of a presentation. Each box in the figure represents one presentation page. Follow along with this figure as you read about each presentation element covered in the rest of this chapter.

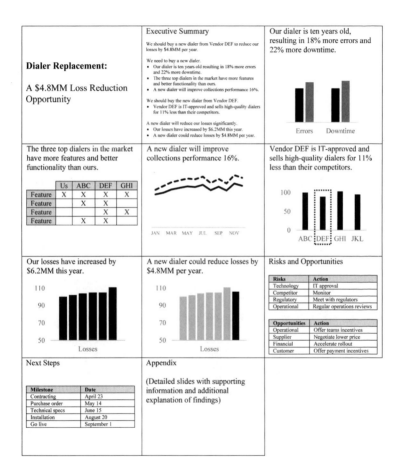

Figure 13.1: The Final Presentation
(Each box represents one slide in the presentation.)

The *Title*

The first element of a good pitch presentation is a title. You'll make many pitches to busy stakeholders. They see dozens of presentations every month. Given how busy they are, they're prioritizing their time and spending it on the biggest, most exciting ideas. Their first assessment of how exciting an idea is comes from their impression of the title. I've seen many terrible presentation titles over the years. Titles like "Market Overview," "Product Launch Update," and "New Complaint Process" fall flat. Based on those titles, you have no idea what the presentation contains or why you should be excited to read it. Candidly, anything with "complaint" and "process" as two-thirds of the title will lead me to bury that pitch at the bottom of the pile! I don't care if it's "new" because it sounds like a painful read. Weak titles, which includes anything entitled "(Blank) Update" or "(Blank) Overview," almost guarantee your stakeholder won't engage with your pitch. Even if they do, their interest in it will be muted because you failed to excite them from the start.

The structured thought process has already provided you with an interesting title. Imagine a title page that, instead of "New Complaint Process," said: "Redesigning Complaint Handling: A \$35MM Process Improvement Opportunity."

Thirty-five million dollars?! I'm reading that! If this title's structure seems familiar, that's because it is. It's the core idea. It contains your recommendation, "We should redesign our complaint handling process," and the button, "because it's worth \$35MM." Your stakeholder should be eager to turn the page because \$35MM focuses on their button. You're getting their attention on the first page.

All you have to do to create a compelling title is modify your core idea so it reads like a title instead of a sentence. Your audience will know exactly what the presentation is about and why it's important for them to read it before they even turn the page. In Figure 13.1 you'll see the title spells out what we're recommending in terms of replacing the dialer and the $4.8MM benefit of making that change. A stakeholder interested in reducing losses will be motivated to flip to page 1 of that pitch because the title grabbed their attention.

The *Executive* Summary

When delivering a pitch, remember you're not writing a mystery novel. Don't make your audience wait to find out what your pitch is about. The executive summary is a great way to let them know what you're pitching right from the start. Your executive summary is the entire pitch on a single page. It should lay out the flow of your presentation. I have more good news for you. You've already written your executive summary! Take the story you proved earlier, copy it, and paste it into your presentation as the first page after your title page. If you had a column-based story, your executive summary will start with your core idea followed by the supporting information contained in your columns. For a layer-based story, your executive summary starts with the "Background" followed by "What's Changed," and ends with your core idea. Like your story, your executive summary should look like a bulleted outline versus being a block of prose. It will be easier for your audience to absorb, and such a summary lends itself nicely to serving as your presentation's table of contents.

Having your entire story on a single page is help-ful for you and your audience. For your audience, they know where the conversation is headed because they have the entire top-level perspective. This enables them to put all the data and information that follows into con-text. Without an executive summary, they're left to as-semble the bigger picture themselves. This is where the executive summary becomes valuable to you. If you don't have one and your audience assembles the bigger picture themselves, you risk them crafting their own story that doesn't match the one you're trying to tell. That can re-sult in them disagreeing with your pitch or asking you to do more analysis to support the new story they've craft-ed because you didn't give them one. Leave nothing to chance. Providing them your executive summary increas-es the likelihood they arrive at the conclusion you want them to which then results in them approving your pitch.

When you share your idea, ideally you'll never get to page 2 of your presentation. If your executive summary is clear enough and your story is compelling enough, you could get approval on the first page. This requires your audience to believe you've been rigorous in your analysis and the pages that follow support all the points in the summary. They'll have to trust you've done the requi-site amount of stakeholder syndication and accounted for their concerns in the presentation's body.

It's possible to achieve the feat of getting your pitch approved on the executive summary page. I know a guy named Angelo who was making a pitch for a $4MM capi-tal investment in a new technology platform. He followed the structured thought process rigorously. His core idea was simple and pushed the stakeholder's button of in-creased profitability. The architecture covered all the required supporting facts and his story laid out the argument in a straightforward manner. He assembled his presentation to include an exciting title and elegant executive summary followed by his supporting analysis. In the pitch meeting, Angelo's stakeholder read the executive summary, nodded, and asked, "Do you have all the analysis to back this up? Have all the stakeholders signed off on your recommendation?" Angelo answered, "Yes to both questions." His stakeholder said, "Okay. I trust you. Since your analysis is always rigorous, I'm ready to approve this. Give me your business case so I can sign it." Angelo handed over the business case, got it signed, and ended the meeting. He didn't go to page 2 because he didn't need to. While this is a rare occurrence, it's possible to achieve once you've built credibility with your stakeholders and you have a reputation for doing all the work required to support your recommendations.

The Presentation *Body*

The main analyses and facts you gathered to support your hypotheses belong in the presentation body. When deciding which facts to include in the main body versus ones to put in the appendix, use the executive summary as a guide. If a point was important enough to belong in the executive summary, it's important enough to have analysis supporting it in the presentation body. If the analysis is only necessary to answer secondary questions that may or may not be asked in the meeting, relegate that analysis to the appendix.

In terms of the sequence of your analyses in the presentation body, follow your executive summary's flow. The analysis supporting the first bullet point in your executive summary should be the first slide after the summary. The executive summary's second bullet point supporting analysis should be the second slide, and so on. Remember, you took the time to refine your story's sequence so it would be easy to follow. Get the benefit of that effort by sequencing your executive summary and the presentation body in the same order. Your audience will have an easier time following along, which makes it easier for them to approve your pitch.

Many presentations include a lead at the top of each slide. The lead is a sentence that tells the audience what they should conclude from the information on the page. If you use leads, copy the corresponding bullet point from your executive summary and paste it on the slide verbatim. Don't change the wording from what you have on the executive summary. First, copying the bullet verbatim will save you the effort of figuring out a new way to say the same thing. Second, the identical wording prevents confusion for your audience because you're not giving them two different interpretations of the same information. From your perspective, you know you're saying the same thing even though you're using different words. Your audience might not share your perspective and could draw different conclusions from the different word choices used on the summary versus the supporting page.

Risks and *Opportunities*

After presenting all the evidence to make your case, I recommend having a page dedicated to risks and opportunities. No pitch is without risk and every pitch has opportunities to deliver more than you're committing to. You should spell out what these possibilities are. Stick to the top three to six risks and three to six opportunities. If you go deeper than that, you might make your contingency list too complex to understand. For each risk, explain the risk's source, the impact if it happens, and how you plan to prevent or mitigate the risk. For each opportunity, define the opportunity, what it's worth, and how you'll try to capture it.

If you don't spell out these risks and opportunities, someone else will. More often than not, your nemesis will enumerate every risk associated with your recommendation. When they do, the other stakeholders in the room can get uncomfortable with approving an idea. They might assume you don't have a well-thought-out risk plan, therefore they won't approve your idea until you present them with one. Conversely, pointing out the risks associated with your idea objectively and proactively can make your audience more comfortable with the pitch. They know you're thinking ahead and have contingency plans in case things go wrong once your recommendation is implemented.

Next *Steps*

Go into your pitch with the belief it will be approved. Let your audience know what you'll do next after they approve your idea. This should not be a massive Gantt chart consisting of a hundred detailed project management tasks. Your next steps should be the three to ten major milestones and actions you'll be taking. Specify the action and the expected timing. If there are specific resources needed for a particular task, identify what they are. This sets an expectation that you'll come to the stakeholder at a defined point in the future for a resource they're committing to provide you when they approve your pitch. When you go to them for that resource, the odds of them giving you what you need are higher than if you don't set the expectation when they're approving your recommendation.

The *Appendix*

During the course of proving and disproving your hypotheses, you'll conduct a substantial amount of analysis. It's a shame to throw away all that work, isn't it? Many times people are tempted to cram all their analysis into the main presentation. They include all the data to demonstrate how rigorous they've been and how hard they've been working. Unfortunately, all that ends up doing is confusing the audience with too much detail. While the analysis was interesting to you, it may not be interesting to your audience. Fortunately, there's a place to put all that information—in the appendix.

The appendix is *your* backup. It's a repository of information you can turn to when you have to answer a more detailed question during your main presentation. You won't provide the appendix to your audience unless they ask for information contained therein. Sometimes people will ask for analytical details underpinning your graphs. Some questions will be about alternate hypotheses you either considered or disproved. Other questions will be idle curiosity or "pet" topics people want to bring up for their own benefit. Whatever the reason for the question, the information in the appendix can answer many of them.

Once you've assembled all these elements, your presentation is complete. As you can see in Figure 13.1, you don't need a long presentation to make your pitch. There are *ten* slides in that example—including the title page! Those ten pages tell a complete story and contain the analyses required to back it up. If people want more detail to support your pitch, you can provide it from the appendix. Now that you've got all your information pulled together, you're ready to make your pitch.

14

Deliver Your *Pitch*

Your pitch delivery is where the structured thought process pays off. You need to make your case in front of the stakeholders who will approve your idea. Whether it's a steering committee of senior executives approving your project, your boss saying yes to your proposed re-organization, or a customer agreeing with the sales pitch you're making, you have to share your idea in a clear and compelling way. While 65% of people are visual learners, approximately 30% are auditory learners who will best absorb your content by hearing you tell them about it. Between your presentation's visuals and the words you speak to accompany it, you've covered the learning styles of the vast majority of people who have to approve your pitch.

Beyond presentation basics like not saying "um" and "uh" or standing in front of the projector, there are techniques related to the structured thought process that will make your pitch concise, understandable, and interesting. The most important tips revolve around how you read your audience, share your information, and answer questions.

Read Your *Audience*

You're holding your pitch meeting for your audience's benefit. Pay attention to them. Instead of focusing your attention on your slides, watch audience reactions to what you say. Read their body language. If you're seeing vigorous head nodding, there's no need to go into detail because they already agree with the point you're making. Move on to the next piece of information. If you're seeing their faces scrunch up on a particular slide, spend time understanding their concerns. Ask them what's on their mind. If they're looking at your slide like a confused dog looking at a ceiling fan, slow down and ask if they have questions.

The better you understand where your audience members are at any given moment, the more effectively you can communicate with and influence them. The best presenters I know rarely look at their slides and instead work hard to forge a connection with audience members. Their slides are there to present complex information visually or to serve as a trigger for them to touch on a specific point. They then talk with the audience about that topic rather than explaining what's on the page.

One of my favorite audience reading stories is about a client of mine. She was going to present to an intimidating member of the company's C-suite. It was a one-on-one meeting. At his request, she had sent her presentation to him a week before the meeting. When she showed up at his door for the meeting, she saw him finish reading the last page of her presentation and turn the page over. He then patted the document twice and motioned for her to come in and join him at his conference table. It was clear to my client that her audience had finished reading everything she had sent him. She had a choice to make: Should she walk him through the document he had finished reading moments ago or do something related to where he was at that instant? She chose the latter. She looked at him and said, "So do you have any questions?"

Her stakeholder smiled and laughed, then said, "Thank you for not forcing me to go through the presentation and for being observant enough to know I had read it. Most people want to drag me through all their content even though I've already seen it. You're one of the first people to ever meet me where I am to have a conversation instead. Yes, I do have questions. Let's go to page 7." They had a wonderful conversation, and he was highly complimentary of her work. The discussion went well because she was smart enough to read her audience and react accordingly. Learn from her example.

Share Information

Send people your presentation before the meeting. Give them at least three days or more to read it if possible. You want them to review the materials before the meeting so the meeting itself can be a dialogue rather than a one-way presentation. Getting the materials beforehand enables them to think through their questions and come prepared to ask them during the meeting. If the first time they see the analysis is in the meeting, the odds of them absorbing all the information and approving your idea the first time they see it are low.

When they've had a chance to think about your pitch for a few days, they'll be better equipped to give you a decision in the actual pitch meeting. In some cases, you'll be able to cancel the meeting entirely. I've had situations where I sent out my pitch presentation a week before the meeting. All the stakeholders wrote back and said they supported the recommendation and approved moving forward. Once the last stakeholder approved the idea via email, I canceled the meeting and used the newfound time to begin implementation of the idea.

If you do end up holding the meeting, remember, you're not there to show off your awesome slide-making skills. You're there to either inform or get approval for a recommendation. Don't take your audience on a forced death march through every slide you've created. First, pare down your slides to the critical few you need for the meeting. This includes cutting out slides that are common knowledge for your audience. This could result in you having multiple versions of a presentation because each one is tailored to a different audience. If you're pitching your idea for product labeling changes to the supply chain team, you need to include the marketing insights analysis. When you make the same pitch to the marketing team, you can leave out the marketing insights pages and put them in the appendix because that audience isn't only familiar with those analyses, they *generated* them!

Only include information your audience needs to have to arrive at your conclusion.

When discussing your slides and analyses, *please* don't read to your audience. Trust me, they're all hooked on phonics. The most common reason presenters read their slides is they're nervous and reading calms their nerves. Instead of reading aloud, cover the major points on the slide and let your audience spend a few moments reading it themselves. The momentary silence will feel uncomfortable for you but I guarantee your audience won't notice the silence because they're preoccupied with reading the slide for themselves. When they finish reading, they'll turn their attention back to you and you can resume the conversation.

Answer *Questions*

Your audience will have questions. Listen to what they're asking. If you're unsure, ask them to clarify what they're asking. You can rephrase the question to them and ask if you've understood them correctly. Once you're clear on the question, answer it directly. Beware of running down analytical rabbit holes and sharing excessive detail. If the answer is 3.25, then tell them the answer is 3.25. Don't explain the calculation you used and the data you pulled to arrive at 3.25. That's not what they asked you. Your task is to keep the conversation on track. Stay focused on the question at hand. Once you've answered their question, confirm with them you've satisfied their request. Say, "Have I answered your question?" and wait for their reply. If they say yes, then proceed with your presentation. If they say no, then ask them what isn't clear in your answer or what additional questions they have.

When answering questions, your appendix will be a powerful source of backup data you can use to address audience concerns. However, when you deliver your pitch, do *not* give out the appendix. You've worked hard to make your presentation simple and short. If you hand out a nice, tight ten-page presentation along with a forty-page appendix, people will flip through every page before you've even introduced yourself. Much to your dismay, you find you're answering a question on page 47 about how you calculated the standard deviation of your market share estimates! You'll lose control of the presentation, and you'll never get back to making your main pitch. Instead, hold the appendix in reserve. If someone asks a question requiring information from the appendix, jump to that particular appendix page, answer the question, and then return to the main presentation. I can almost guarantee you won't make too many trips to the appendix if you've been rigorous about applying the structured thought process because all the most important information will already be in the main part of your presentation.

Close the *Deal*

The reason you made the pitch in the first place was to get approval. Once you've finished presenting and answering everyone's questions, explicitly ask for approval for your idea. Get the decision makers in the room to commit to moving forward. If you don't, you run the risk of people leaving the room with a different understanding of whether or not your idea was given a green light to proceed. You can follow up the meeting with an email to participants recapping the conversation and asking them to confirm via email they approve of moving forward.

Having explicit documentation that your idea was approved can smooth over misunderstandings that might arise.

Next Steps for *Using* the Structured Thought Process

The structured thought process is a powerful method for generating compelling recommendations that get approved. To get the most out of the method, apply it regularly. I suggest you pick a mid-sized recommendation you're making and use the process to build your case. Ideally, you'll have anywhere from two to four months between the time you decide to apply the method and the day your recommendation is due. That will give you plenty of time to get familiar with the method. A mid-sized project is a good choice because you'll get practice managing complexity without being overwhelmed. Two to four months allows time for you to apply the method without rushing and leaves a buffer for recovering from mistakes you might make.

You can get more practice with the structured thought process by applying it to smaller communications. Get in the habit of structuring your emails. Think through your core idea and decide whether to write the email in a layer or column architecture. Be clear about the story you're trying to tell in the email. Look at previous emails you've sent and rework them using the structured thought process—especially if your first email didn't receive a favorable response. The more you use the method, the easier it will be to apply it to all your communications.

When you apply the method, be disciplined! Resist the urge to dive into the data before you've created your architecture or written your story. Those steps provide the greatest benefit. Going straight to the data defeats the purpose of using the method. Follow the steps in order and be open to iterating through the process as required. The first few times you use the method, it may feel intellectually uncomfortable. But the more you use it, the more natural it will feel. Before you know it, you'll be thinking in terms of architecture rather than getting pulled into the details. Once you reach that point, you'll find you're generating recommendations more quickly, having fewer approval meetings, doing less irrelevant analysis, and being more successful at getting your ideas approved.

For the last twelve years, my day job has been teaching people how to use the structured thought process. I've taught the method around the world to thousands of people in a variety of industries and functions. Whether it's via classroom training, video-based courses, individual coaching, or this book, I love showing others how to use this efficient and effective approach to getting ideas approved. To learn about the help my firm can provide, visit *www.elegantpitch.com/course/* where you can find details on the program. While this method itself is simple, applying it is far from easy. It takes discipline, practice, guidance, and feedback. I'd welcome the opportunity to teach you how to incorporate the structured thought process into your daily work routine because I know how much time and effort can be saved through the application of this approach.

Remember, a successful pitch isn't about smothering people in data and hoping they're overwhelmed by how rigorous you've been in your analysis. Creating an *elegant* pitch requires you to think through your objectives, consider your audience's goals, and then craft a straightforward recommendation that's easy to approve. The structured thought process is your key to making every pitch you deliver clear, concise, and compelling.

Index

About the *Author*

Mike Figliuolo is an honor graduate of the United States Military Academy at West Point, where he graduated in the top 5 percent of his class. He served in the U.S. Army as an armor officer. After several years of leading soldiers in the army, Mike spent time in corporate America as a consultant at McKinsey & Company and as an executive in various roles at Capital One Financial and the Scotts Miracle-Gro Company.

Mike is the founder and managing director of *thought*LEADERS, LLC (*www.thoughtleadersllc.com*). He and his team train leaders at world-class companies on topics of leadership, strategy, communications, innovation, and other critical business skills. He's the author of *One Piece of Paper: The Simple Approach to Powerful, Personal Leadership*, a book that shows leaders how to be authentic by sharing their personal story on a single page. He's also the coauthor of *Lead Inside the Box: How Smart Leaders Guide Their Teams to Exceptional Results*. A highly sought-after speaker and trainer, Mike has delivered his message to thousands of leaders around the world through keynote presentations, classroom instruction, and personal coaching.

Mike's clients include Abbott, Discover, Google, OhioHealth, Visa, Heinz, Abbvie, Cardinal Health, Huntington, Bristol-Myers Squibb, Nationwide, and many other industry-leading firms.